Better Homes and Gardens®

WOOD™
LARGE FURNITURE
YOU CAN MAKE

WE CARE!

All of us at Meredith® Books are dedicated to giving you the
information and ideas you need to create beautiful and useful
woodworking projects. We guarantee your satisfaction with this
book for as long as you own it. We also welcome your comments
and suggestions. Please write us at Meredith® Books, LS-356LF,
1716 Locust St., Des Moines, IA 50336.

A **WOOD**™ **BOOK**
Published by Meredith® Books

MEREDITH® BOOKS
Vice President, Editorial Director: Elizabeth P. Rice
Art Director: Ernest Shelton
Managing Editor: David A. Kirchner
Project Editors: James D. Blume, Marsha Jahns
Project Managers: Liz Anderson,
    Jennifer Speer Ramundt, Angela K. Renkoski

Associate Art Directors: Neoma Thomas,
    Linda Ford Vermie, Randall Yontz
Assistant Art Directors: Lynda Haupert, Harijs Priekulis,
    Tom Wegner
Graphic Designers: Mary Schlueter Bendgen,
    Michael Burns, Mick Schnepf
Art Production: Director, John Berg; Associate, Joe Heuer;
    Office Manager, Michaela Lester

President, Book Group: James F. Stack
Vice President, Retail Marketing: Jamie L. Martin
Vice President, Administrative Services: Rick Rundall

WOOD® MAGAZINE
President, Magazine Group: James A. Autry
Editorial Director: Doris Eby
Editor: Larry Clayton

MEREDITH CORPORATION OFFICERS
Chairman of the Executive Committee: E. T. Meredith III
Chairman of the Board: Robert A. Burnett
President and Chief Executive Officer: Jack D. Rehm

LARGE FURNITURE YOU CAN MAKE
Project Editor: James D. Blume
Contributing Project Editor: James A. Hufnagel
Contributing How-To Editor: Marlen Kemmet
Graphic Designers: Michael Burns, Tom Wegner
Project Manager: Jennifer Speer Ramundt
Contributing Text Editor: Barbara L. Klein
Publishing Systems Text Processor: Paula Forest

Special thanks to Kathy Stevens

On the front cover: Modular Entertainment Center,
    pages 15–21
On the back cover (clockwise from top left):
    Expandable Oak Dining Table and Chairs, pages 37–47;
    Barrister's Bookcase, pages 5–9; Solid-Oak Settee,
    pages 67–73

Meredith® Books also publishes Better Homes and Gardens® Books,
Country Home™ Books, Meredith® Press Books, and Sedgewood®
Press Books.

STORAGE UNITS

Because no home ever seems to have quite enough storage space, we've designed five projects that can help you get things organized around your house.

BARRISTER'S BOOKCASE

L ong ago, attorneys serving in England's Superior Court became known as barristers. And like all good lawyers, these chaps had an ever-increasing need for practical, yet attractive, book storage. Their solution: the barrister's bookcase.

Like the originals, our units, shown *opposite,* are stackable. Build one or two cabinets now, and add more cabinets as your storage needs expand.

And don't forget to take a look at our matching file cabinet on pages 10–14. The two make a terrific duo.

Note: The instructions explain how to make the components for one cabinet, one cabinet door, one base, and one top. The Bill of Materials, page 7, also gives the number of pieces for a single cabinet, door, base, and top. If you plan to make more than one cabinet, we suggest you cut all identical pieces at the same time to ensure uniformity.

Build the cabinet frames

1. Cut the back, side, and bottom-frame members (A–F) to the sizes listed in the Bill of Materials. (We ripped all the stock for parts A through F at the same time.)

2. Attach a ¼" dado blade to the tablesaw arbor. Raise the blade ⅜" above the surface of the saw table. Cut a ¼" groove in the center of *one* edge the length of each back-frame member (A, B) and each side-frame member (C, D) as shown in photo A, *upper right.* (We first test-cut the ¼" groove in scrap stock the same thickness as the rails and stiles until we had the groove accurately centered. Also, use the scrap stock to verify that the dado blade is set at the correct height [⅜"] before cutting the actual cabinet-frame members.)

3. To cut the stub tenons on the ends of parts B and D, position the auxiliary wood fence (attached to your rip fence) ⅜" from the outside edge of the dado blade as shown in photo B, *below.* Position the blade so it is ¼" above the surface of the saw table. Now, using a miter gauge for support, cut the rabbets on both faces of each end of the parts as dimensioned on the Stub Tenon Detail accompanying the Cabinet Drawing, page 6. Again, test-cut scrap stock first, and check the fit of the tenon in the ¼"-wide groove.

Cut the ⅜"-deep groove with a ¼" dado blade on the tablesaw.

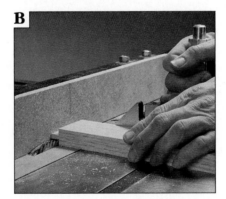

Use a miter gauge and auxiliary wood fence when cutting the stub tenons on your tablesaw.

4. Cut the back panel (G), the two end panels (H), and the bottom panel (I) to size from ¼" oak plywood. (After cutting the plywood panels to the sizes stated in the Bill of Materials, we trimmed the back and end panels a fraction. This makes for a slightly loose fit of the panels in the frame, and allows for expansion of the frame members. Too tight a fit might force the frame-member joints to separate later.) Next, dry-clamp the side and back frames with the plywood panels in place to check the fit. Glue and clamp the end and back frames together, checking each frame for square. (To prevent the plywood panels from rattling in the frames, we used silicone sealant to hold them in place.)

5. For the bottom frame, dry-clamp parts E and F together. Mark the dowel-hole centerpoints where dimensioned on the Rabbet and Hole Detail accompanying the Cabinet Drawing. Remove the clamps, and drill ⅜" holes 1¹⁄₁₆" deep in the mating parts where marked. (We used a doweling jig when drilling the holes and dowel centers to transfer the hole locations to the mating parts.) Using ⅜" dowel pins 2" long, glue and clamp the bottom frame together, checking for square.

6. Sand the top face of the bottom frame smooth. Using a ⅜" rabbet bit, rout a rabbet ¼" deep along the top inside edge of the bottom frame. Square the round corners with a chisel. Glue and clamp the bottom plywood panel (I) in the bottom rabbeted frame. Wipe off any excess glue immediately with a damp cloth.

7. Finish-sand all four frames, being careful not to sand through the thin oak-veneer surface.

continued

BARRISTER'S BOOKCASE
continued

ROUTER TEMPLATE

Assemble the frames to form the cabinet

1. Using the Router Template Drawing at *left* as a guide, cut the router template to rectangular size (7×19″) from ¼″ stock. (We cut ours to size from a scrap piece of ¼″ hardboard.) Now carefully lay out, mark, and cut the 1½×13⅛6″ notch along the bottom edge of the ¼″ stock.

2. Fit your router base with a ⅝″ bushing and a ⅜″ straight bit. (Our bushing was too long, so we cut it with a hacksaw until it protruded a fraction less than ¼″ below the surface of the router base.) Clamp the template to the top of an end frame with the *top* and *front* edges flush where shown on the Router Template Drawing. Then rout a ⅜″ groove ¼″ deep. Repeat this procedure for the other end frame.

3. Cut the cabinet's front rail (J) to size from ¾″ oak stock.

Note: The hinge-pin grooves in the end frames must be a mirror image of each other. Lay the frames side by side, as shown at *right,* so you don't rout the grooves in the same position on each.

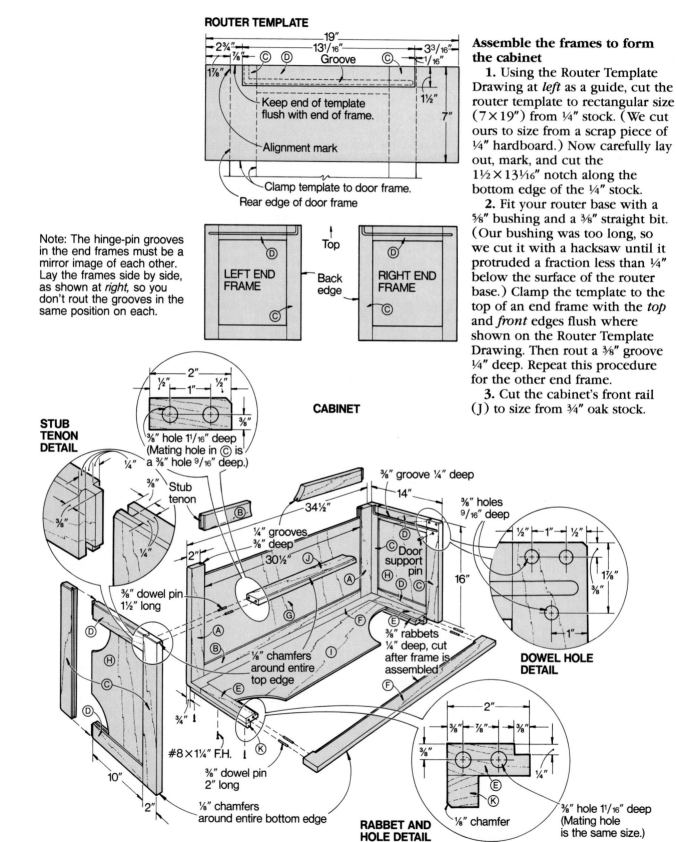

Bill of Materials

Part	Finished Size*			Mat.	Qty.
	T	W	L		
Cabinet					
A back stile	¾"	2"	16"	O	2
B back rail	¾"	2"	31¼"	O	2
C side stile	¾"	2"	16"	O	4
D side rail	¾"	2"	10¾"	O	4
E bottom stile	¾"	2"	9¼"	O	2
F bottom rail	¾"	2"	34½"	O	2
G* back panel	¼"	31¼"	12¾"	OP	1
H end panel	¼"	10¾"	12¾"	OP	2
I bottom panel	¼"	10"	31¼"	OP	1
J front rail	¾"	2"	34½"	O	1
K alignmt. block	¾"	¾"	11¼"	O	2

*Part marked with an * is 31¼" wide by 12¾" long. Measure width across the grain; the length is measured with the grain. See the Cutting Diagram, *below*, for layout.

Part	Finished Size			Mat.	Qty.
	T	W	L		
Door					
L stile	¾"	2"	14¼"	O	2
M rail	¾"	2"	30¼"	O	2
N glass stop	¼"	⅜"	30¼"	O	2
O glass stop	¼"	⅜"	11"	O	2
Top					
P front/back	¾"	2"	34½"	O	2
Q end	¾"	2½"	12½"	O	2
R decorative end	¾"	2"	14¾"	O	2
S panel	¼"	13¼"	34½"	OP	1
Base					
T front/back	¾"	4"	34½"	O	2
U end	¾"	4"	14¾"	O	2

Material Key: O—oak, OP—oak plywood.
Supplies: ⅜" dowel pins 1½" long, ⅜" dowel pins 2" long, ⅜" dowel stock (no glue groove), ⅛"-thick glass for door, #8×1¼" flathead wood screws, #8×1¾" flathead wood screws, #17×¾" brads, carbon paper, ¼" hardboard for template, silicone sealant, paraffin, stain, finish.

Cutting Diagram

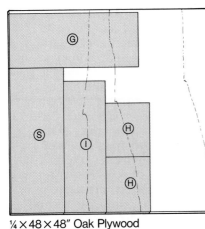

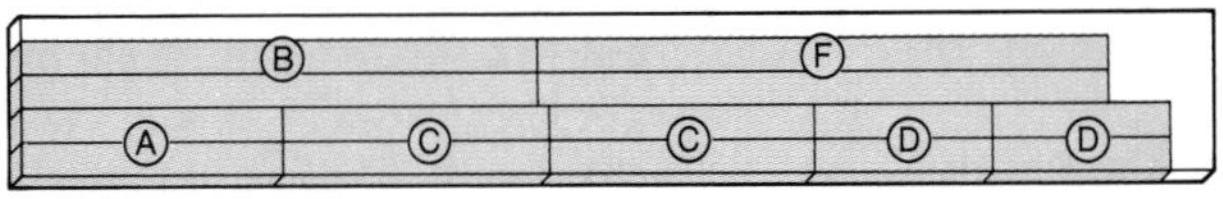

¾×9¼×72" Oak

¼×48×48" Oak Plywood

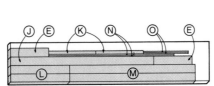

¾×9¼×48" Oak

¾×9¼×96" Oak

4. Using the Dowel Hole Detail accompanying the Cabinet Drawing, *opposite, bottom,* as a guide, lay out and drill three ⅜" holes 9/16" deep in the upper front corner of each end frame.

5. Now, using the dimensions on the Cabinet Drawing, lay out and drill a pair of ⅜" holes 1¹/₁₆" deep in each end of the front rail (J). (If you have them, you could use a pair of ⅜" dowel centers to transfer the hole positions to the ends of the front rail.)

6. Using the Cabinet Drawing as a guide, glue and clamp the back frame to the bottom frame, checking for square. Keep the bottom edge of the back frame flush with the bottom face of the bottom frame. Wipe off any excess glue with a damp cloth.

7. Glue two ⅜×1½" dowel pins in the holes in each end of the front rail (J). Aligning the bottom edges of the end frames flush with the bottom face of the bottom frame, glue and clamp the end frames and front rail to the back/bottom-frame assembly. Check for square. Wipe off any excess glue with a damp cloth, or scrape it off after it dries.

8. Cut two ⅜" dowels 1" long. Glue one dowel in the remaining hole on each end frame where shown on the Cabinet Drawing. (These pins support the door horizontally when you open it. They also force the top of the door to align flush with cabinet front when the door is closed.)

9. Using a chamfer bit, rout a ⅛" chamfer along all top outside edges of the cabinet.

10. Cut the two alignment blocks (K) to size. Rout or sand a chamfer along one edge of each. Screw them (no glue) to the bottom of the bottom frame, ¾" in from the back edge and flush with the outside edge of E (not D). The chamfer should be on the *bottom* facing *out.* (The alignment blocks center and hold the cabinet on the base so all outside surfaces are flush. Using screws and no glue allows you to realign them if necessary.)

continued

BARRISTER'S BOOKCASE
continued

Make the cabinet door

1. Cut the stiles (L) and rails (M) to size. Dry-clamp the door frame together. Then, using the dimensions on the Dowel Hole Detail accompanying the Cabinet Door Drawing at *right,* mark the dowel-hole reference lines on the frame. Remove the clamps, and drill ⅜″ holes 1¹⁄₁₆″ deep where marked. Use a doweling jig for proper alignment and ⅜″ dowel centers to transfer the hole positions to the mating piece.

2. Glue, dowel, and clamp the door frame together. Check for square and flatness as you work.

3. Sand the door smooth. Mount a ⅜″ rabbet bit into your router. Then, with the *front* of the door facing *down,* rout a ⅜″ rabbet ⅜″ deep along the back inside edge of the door frame for the glass. Square the rabbet corners with a chisel.

4. Rout a ³⁄₁₆″ chamfer along the front edges of the door frame where shown on the Cabinet Door Drawing.

5. Drill a ¼″ hole 5″ from each end where shown on the Cabinet Door Drawing for mounting the wooden knobs later.

6. Cut the glass stops (N, O).

7. Lay out and drill a ⅜″ hole ¾″ deep ⅜″ down from the top edge on each end of the door frame where shown on the Cabinet Door Drawing. Cut two 1″-long dowels from ⅜″ dowel stock. Glue the dowels into the ⅜″ holes you just drilled. Check that the dowels protrude no more than ¼″; sand down if necessary. Then sand a slight round-over on the protruding end of each dowel. Doing this enables the door to track smoothly in the hinge pin grooves.

8. Rip or joint a 5° bevel along the bottom edge of the door frame where shown on the Dowel Hole Detail.

9. Lay out and drill a ⁵⁄₁₆″ hole ⅜″ deep 1″ from the bottom of

CABINET DOOR

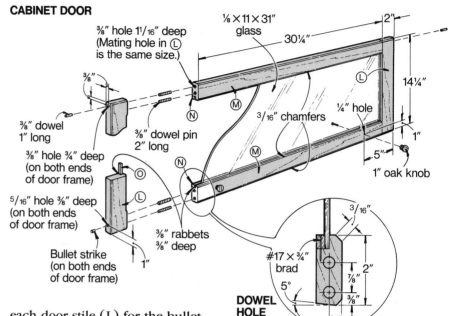

⅜″ hole 1¹⁄₁₆″ deep (Mating hole in ⓛ is the same size.)

⅛ × 11 × 31″ glass

30¼″

2″

⅜″

⒩

Ⓜ

³⁄₁₆″ chamfers

¼″ hole

14¼″

⅜″ dowel 1″ long

⅜″ dowel pin 2″ long

⒩

Ⓜ

ⓛ

5″

1″

1″ oak knob

⅜″ hole ¾″ deep (on both ends of door frame)

⁵⁄₁₆″ hole ⅜″ deep (on both ends of door frame)

Ⓞ

ⓛ

⅜″ rabbets ⅜″ deep

Bullet strike (on both ends of door frame)

1″

DOWEL HOLE DETAIL

³⁄₁₆″

#17 × ¾″ brad

5°

2″

⅞″

⅜″

⅜″

each door stile (L) for the bullet strike (see the Cabinet Door Drawing). Install the strikes.

10. Lower the door frame into the hinge-pin grooves in the end frames, and close the door. With the front of the door flush with the front of the cabinet, mark the position, and nail the catch plates to the inside edges of the cabinet frame where shown on the drawing *below.* Locate carefully; the door should align with the cabinet front.

Construct the cabinet top

1. Cut the front and back pieces (P), end pieces (Q), and decorative end pieces (R) to width and length. Mark and cut the ⅞ × 1¼″ notch in the front of

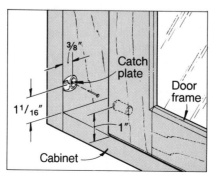

⅜″

Catch plate

Door frame

1¹⁄₁₆″

1″

Cabinet

each end piece (see the Cabinet Top Drawing, *opposite, top*).

2. Using carbon paper, transfer the Full-Sized Pattern accompanying the Cabinet Top Drawing to the front end of each decorative end piece. Cut the marked fronts to shape on a bandsaw, and sand smooth.

3. Cut or rout a ⅜″ rabbet ¼″ deep along the top inside edge of the front and back pieces (P).

4. Dry-clamp the cabinet top (P, Q, R) together, and check the fit of the top on the cabinet. (When clamping the pieces, make sure that the *top* edges of the end pieces [Q] align flush with the *bottom* edges of the rabbet in the front and back pieces.) When checking the fit of the top on the cabinet, check to see that all edges are flush. Remove the clamps, and trim if necessary. Glue and clamp the top assembly together, checking for square.

5. Measure the rabbeted opening, and cut the plywood panel (S) to fit snugly inside the ¼″-deep rabbet. Glue and clamp the panel in position.

CABINET TOP

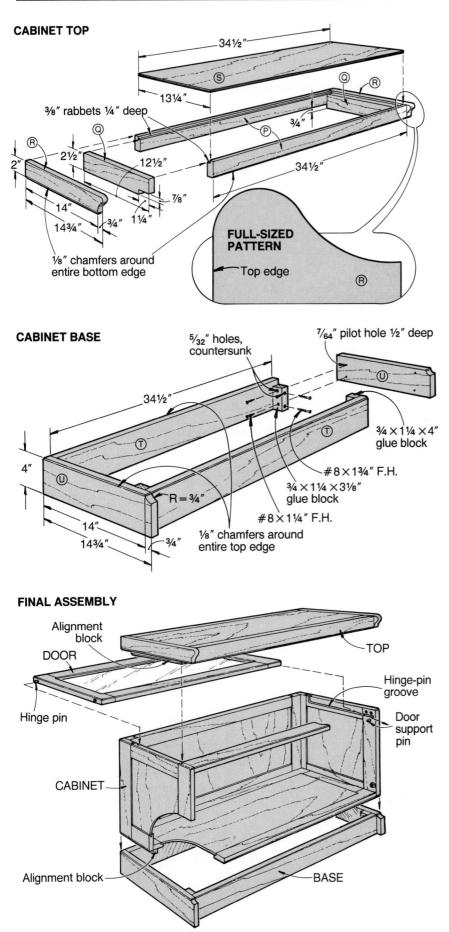

34½"

13¼"

⅜" rabbets ¼" deep

S
Q
R
Q
P
R
R

¾"

34½"

2½"

12½"

2"

14"

¾"

⅛" chamfers around entire bottom edge

7⁄8"

1¼"

14¾"

FULL-SIZED PATTERN

Top edge

R

CABINET BASE

5⁄32" holes, countersunk

7⁄64" pilot hole ½" deep

34½"

U

T

T

¾ × 1¼ × 4" glue block

#8 × 1¾" F.H.

4"

U

¾ × 1¼ × 3⅛" glue block

#8 × 1¼" F.H.

R = ¾"

14"

14¾"

¾"

⅛" chamfers around entire top edge

FINAL ASSEMBLY

Alignment block

DOOR

TOP

Hinge-pin groove

Hinge pin

Door support pin

CABINET

Alignment block

BASE

6. Rout a ⅛" chamfer along the entire bottom edge of the cabinet top to match the chamfer on the top of the cabinet.

Build the base

1. Cut the front and back (T) and the end pieces (U) to size. Now cut the four glue blocks to the sizes stated on the Cabinet Base Drawing, *left, middle.*

2. Mark and cut a ¾" radius on the end pieces' front top corners.

3. Drill and countersink 5⁄32" holes in the glue blocks. Glue and screw the glue blocks to the front and back pieces (T), flush with their ends. Next, glue and screw the end pieces (U) to the front and back pieces.

4. Rout a ⅛" chamfer around the top edge of the base where shown on the drawing.

Assemble and finish

1. Stack the components, and sand the outside surfaces flush. Unstack. Sand each component.

2. Mask off the bullet catch hardware. Stain and finish all the pieces (including the glass stops and knobs) as desired.

3. Have glass cut to size for the door. Position the glass and glass stops (N, O) in the rabbet, and drive brads to secure the stops. (To avoid splitting the oak, we predrilled holes in the stops using one of the brads as a drill bit.)

4. Apply paraffin to the hinge pins (⅜" dowels) and the inside edges of the hinge-pin grooves.

5. Remove the masking from the hardware, attach the knobs, and stack the units.

Buying Guide

• **Bullet catches.** Complete with strikes and pins. 5⁄16" diameter by ⅜" long, catalog no. 28472. For current price, contact The Woodworkers' Store, 21801 Industrial Blvd., Rogers, MN 55374-9514. Or call 612/428-2199.

• **Oak knobs.** 1" diameter, catalog no. 36616, 2 needed for each cabinet. Contact The Woodworkers' Store at the address or phone number above.

STACKABLE FILE CABINET

No matter how large our desks, most of us always seem to need more space, especially for filing. If you face the same space problem in your home or office, why not solve it with our stackable file cabinet? Made of oak—like the classic file cabinets of old—it matches the barrister's bookcase on pages 4–9 in design and construction.

The double file cabinet, *left*, measures 15″ wide by 24″ deep by 30″ high. If you don't need the extra worktop surface, but do need extra room for your papers, make the file cabinet four or five units high.

Note: The techniques used to build the file cabinet are quite similar to those used to make the barrister's bookcase. To avoid duplication, we'll be referring to some of the instructions and photos for that project.

The instructions explain how to make the components for one cabinet carcass, one file drawer, one top, and one base, and the Bill of Materials, opposite, gives the number of pieces required for the same components. If you're making more than one cabinet carcass and drawer, we suggest you cut all identical pieces at the same time to ensure uniformity.

Start with the cabinet carcass

1. Cut the back-frame stiles (A) and rails (B) to the sizes listed in the Bill of Materials. Then cut the side-frame and bottom-frame stiles and rails (C, D, E, F) to size.

2. Attach a ¼″ dado blade to the tablesaw. Raise the blade ⅜″ above the surface of the saw table. As shown in photo A of the bookcase project, page 5, cut a ¼″ groove, centered from side to side, along one edge the length of each part. (We test-cut the groove in scrap stock the same thickness as the rails and stiles to ensure it was centered.)

3. To cut the stub tenons on the ends of parts B, D, and E, reposition the auxiliary rip fence next to the dado blade as shown in photo B, page 5. Position the blade ¼″ above the surface of the saw table. Using a miter gauge, cut a ⅜″ rabbet ¼″ deep on both faces of each end of the parts to form the stub tenon (see the Stub Tenon Top View accompanying the Cabinet Carcass Drawing, *opposite*).

4. Cut the back panel (G), side panels (H), and bottom panel (I) to size from ¼″ oak plywood. Dry-clamp the frames together.

The plywood panels should fit a bit loosely to allow for frame movement; trim the plywood, if it's snug.

5. Glue and clamp the four individual frames together, checking for square. (We ran a small bead of silicone sealant in the back- and side-frame grooves to keep the plywood panels from rattling later.) Sand each frame.

6. Cut the front rail (J) to size.

7. Using the dimensions on the Cabinet Carcass Drawing, mark the location of, *continued*

CABINET CARCASS

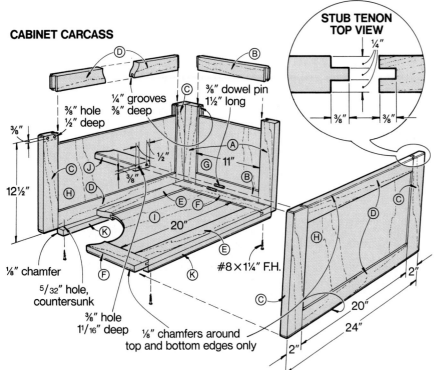

- ¼" grooves ⅜" deep
- ⅜" hole ½" deep
- ⅜" dowel pin 1½" long
- ⅜"
- 12½"
- ½"
- ⅜"
- 11"
- 20"
- ⅛" chamfer
- 5/32" hole, countersunk
- ⅜" hole 1¹/₁₆" deep
- ⅛" chamfers around top and bottom edges only
- #8 × 1¼" F.H.
- 2"
- 20"
- 24"
- 2"

STUB TENON TOP VIEW
- ¼"
- ⅜"
- ⅜"

Cutting Diagram

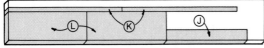

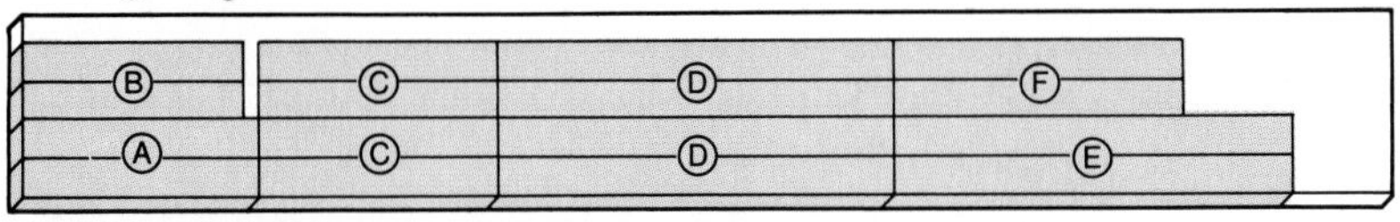

¾ × 9¼ × 72" Oak

(B) (C) (D) (F)
(A) (C) (D) (E)

(L) (K) (J)

¾ × 7¼ × 48" Oak

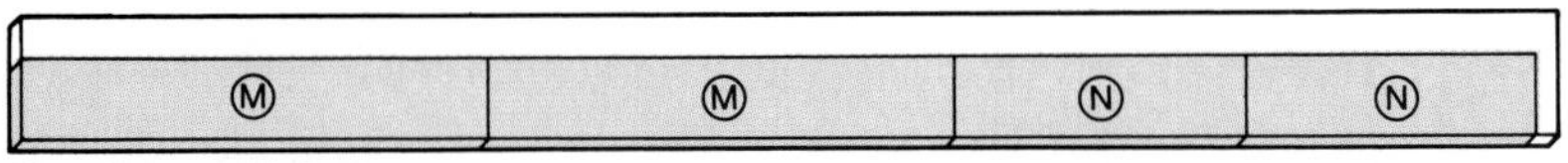

(M) (M) (N) (N)

½ × 5½ × 72" Oak

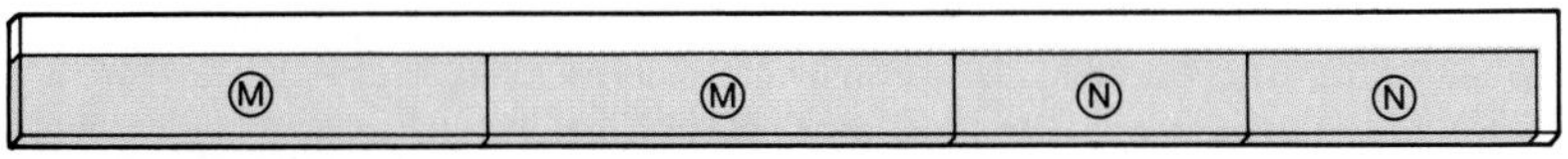

(M) (M) (N) (N)

½ × 5½ × 72" Oak

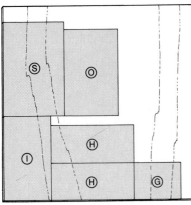

(S) (O)
(H)
(I) (H) (G)

¼ × 48 × 48" Oak Plywood

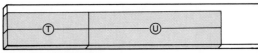

(T) (U)

¾ × 7¼ × 48" Oak

(Q) (P) (R)

¾ × 5½ × 72" Oak

Bill of Materials

Part	Finished Size			Mat.	Qty.
	T	W	L		
File Enclosure					
A back stile	¾"	2"	12½"	O	2
B back rail	¾"	2"	11¾"	O	2
C side stile	¾"	2"	12½"	O	4
D side rail	¾"	2"	20¾"	O	4
E bottom rail	¾"	2"	20¾"	O	2
F bottom stile	¾"	1⅝"	15"	O	2
G back panel	¼"	11¾"	9¼"	OP	1
H side panel	¼"	20¾"	9¼"	OP	2
I bottom panel	¼"	11¾"	20¾"	OP	1
J front rail	¾"	2"	15"	O	1
K alignmt. block	¾"	¾"	21¼"	O	2
Drawer					
L false front	¾"	10¾"	14¾"	O	1
M side	½"	7½"	22"	O	2
N front/ back	½"	7½"	13½"	O	2
O bottom	¼"	13½"	21½"	OP	1
Top					
P front/ back	¾"	2"	15"	O	2
Q side	¾"	2½"	22½"	O	2
R decorative side	¾"	2"	24¾"	O	2
S panel	¼"	15"	23¼"	OP	1
Base					
T front/ back	¾"	3"	15"	O	2
U side	¾"	3"	24¾"	O	2

Material Key: O—oak, OP—oak plywood.
Supplies: #8 × 1" flathead wood screws, #8 × 1¼" flathead wood screws, #8 × 1¾" flathead wood screws, ⅜ × 1½" dowel pins, #4 finish nails, stain, finish.

STACKABLE FILE CABINET
continued

then drill, a pair of ⅜" holes 1¹⁄₁₆" deep in each end of the front rail. (We used a doweling jig when drilling the holes.) Using dowel centers, transfer the hole locations in the front rail to the top front corner of each side frame. Drill ⅜" holes ½" deep where marked by the dowel centers.

8. Glue and clamp the back frame to the bottom frame, checking for square. Later, remove the clamps, and glue and clamp the side frames and front rail to the back/bottom-frame assembly. Make sure all edges are flush, and wipe off any excess glue with a damp cloth.

9. Rout a chamfer along the top and bottom edges of the cabinet.

10. Cut the two alignment blocks (K) to size. Rout a ⅛" chamfer along one edge of each block. Screw them (no glue) to the bottom of the bottom frame ¾" in from the back edge, ¾" from the side edges, and with the chamfered edge facing down and out. (The alignment blocks center the cabinet over the base.)

Build the file drawer

1. Cut the false drawer front (L) to size. (We glued up narrower stock to achieve the 10¾" width.)

2. To form the chamfer on the drawer front, start by raising the tablesaw blade ⅛" above the surface of the saw table, and position the rip fence 1⅜" away from the outside edge of the blade. (See the Panel Section Drawing, *center right.*) Make a cut along each edge of the panel where shown on the Kerf Location Drawing, *lower right.* To cut the bevels, position the rip fence ⁷⁄₁₆" from the inside edge of the blade at table level. Raise the tablesaw blade 1¼" above the surface of the saw table, and tilt the blade 10° from center. Then make the four cuts on the false

DRAWER

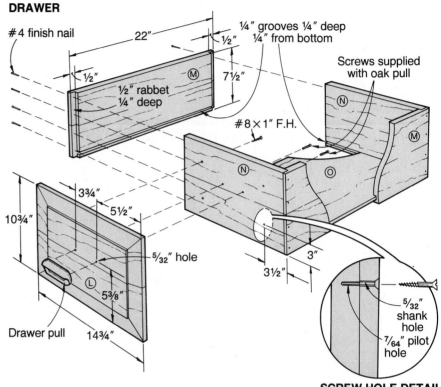

SCREW HOLE DETAIL

PANEL SECTION

KERF LOCATION

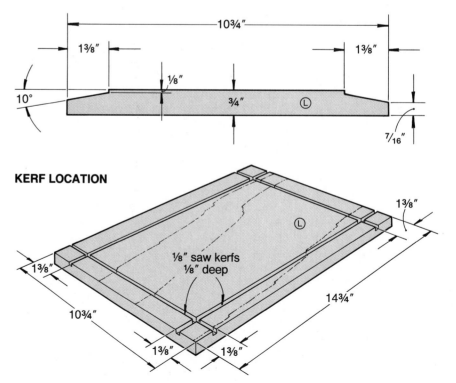

Cut the relief kerfs first; then bevel-cut the drawer front with the blade tilted to 10°.

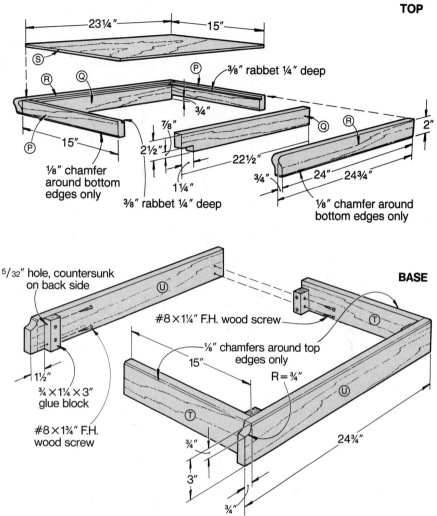

TOP

23¼"   15"

S

3/8" rabbet ¼" deep

R   Q   P

¾"

7/8"

P   Q   R   2"

15"

1/8" chamfer around bottom edges only

2½"

22½"

¾"   24"   24¾"

1¼"

3/8" rabbet ¼" deep

1/8" chamfer around bottom edges only

BASE

5/32" hole, countersunk on back side

U

#8×1¼" F.H. wood screw

T

1½"

¾ × 1¼ × 3" glue block

#8×1¾" F.H. wood screw

1/8" chamfers around top edges only

15"

R = ¾"

T   U

¾"

24¾"

3"

¾"

drawer front as shown in photo A *above.* Sand the beveled surfaces.

3. Cut the drawer sides (M) and front and back panels (N) to size from ½" oak. (Edge-join stock to achieve the required width.) Cut the drawer bottom (O) to size.

4. Using your tablesaw and dado blade, cut a ¼" groove, ¼" deep, ¼" from the bottom edge of the drawer sides and front and back panels where shown on the Drawer Drawing, *opposite, top.* With a ½" dado blade, cut a ½" rabbet ¼" deep along the front and back panels of the drawer sides (M) where shown on the drawing.

5. Dry-clamp the drawer together (without the false front), checking for square and a good fit of the drawer bottom (O).

6. Glue and nail the drawer together (without the false front). Do not nail into the drawer bottom; it should float loosely in the groove.

Construct the top

To build the cabinet top, refer to the Top Drawing, *upper right;* the dimensions for the top given in the Bill of Materials, page 11; and the instructions for the bookcase top, pages 8 and 9.

Build the base

To build the cabinet base, refer to the Base Drawing, *center right;* the dimensions for the base given in the Bill of Materials, page 11; and the instructions for the bookcase base, page 9.

Install the drawer slides

Note: Each drawer slide consists of two basic parts (plus the screws)—the telescoping section you attach to the cabinet carcass and the drawer mount that attaches to the drawer.

1. Place the left telescoping section against the left side of the cabinet interior. Fasten the left telescoping section ¾" back from the front edge of the cabinet (see the Final Assembly Drawing, page 14). Fasten the right telescoping section the same way.

2. Cut three spacers measuring 1" wide by 12" long. Position the spacers under the drawer in front of the file enclosure as shown in photo B, page 14.

3. Extend the telescoping sections flush with the front of the drawer. Fit one end of the drawer mount into the hook on the top of the tail end of each telescoping section as shown in photo B. Lower the drawer mount down onto the black clip on each telescoping section. Screw the drawer mount to the drawer side, flush with the front (see photo C, page 14).

4. To attach the false drawer front (L) to the drawer, start by placing a piece of double-faced tape on the front face of the drawer front (N). Position the false front against the drawer front. Center it in the cabinet carcass opening from side to side and top to bottom. When correctly positioned,   *continued*

STACKABLE FILE CABINET
continued

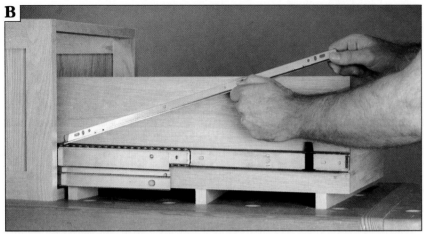

B

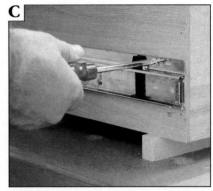

C

Elevate the drawer to the correct height; then screw the drawer mount to the side of the drawer.

To mount the slide, attach the drawer mount to the rear hook on the telescoping section, and lower it onto the black clip at the front of the telescoping section.

squeeze the two together. Carefully extend the drawer from the cabinet carcass, and clamp the false front to the drawer front to ensure that it doesn't move. Using the hole sizes stated on the Screw Hole Detail accompanying the Drawer Drawing, page 12, drill and screw the false front to the drawer front. Finally, drill two ⁵⁄₃₂" holes through the drawer front assembly for the drawer pulls.

Complete the assembly

1. Stack the assemblies, adjust the alignment blocks, if necessary, and sand the outside surfaces flush. Now disassemble the components, and sand each.

2. Stain and finish as desired. Reassemble all parts and attach the drawer pull.

Note: For added stability when stacking several drawers, you might consider securing the sections together in the back with ½ × 3" brass mending plates or with metal angle brackets.

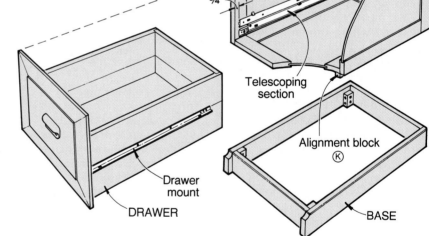

FINAL ASSEMBLY

TOP

CABINET CARCASS

¾"

Telescoping section

Alignment block Ⓚ

Drawer mount

DRAWER

BASE

Buying Guide
• **Drawer pull.** Surface-mounted, unfinished oak, 4½" wide by 1¾" high. Mounts from rear with machine screws, which are included. Catalog no. 33316. For current price, contact The Woodworkers' Store, 21801 Industrial Blvd., Rogers, MN 55374-9514. Or call 612/428-2199.

• **Full-extension slide.** Ball-bearing construction, zinc-plated cold-rolled steel, 22" long, catalog no. 32649. Contact The Woodworkers' Store at the address or phone number at left.

MODULAR ENTERTAINMENT CENTER

W ith just a power saw, router, and palm sander, Gary Schuknecht, of Troutdale, Oregon, set out to build an entertainment center in his garage workshop. When he finished, Gary knew he had a top-notch design.

"We needed an entertainment center for our stereo, TV, records, videotapes, and magazines," Gary told us. "I designed the units plenty deep so the TV and turntable wouldn't stick out the front. My wife, Linda, claims this is the nicest woodworking project I've ever made."

We liked Gary's design so well that we decided to build three sections ourselves and then share his design with you. Start modestly and build just one unit, or if you have the materials, build all three.

Note: The three-unit entertainment center shown at right *consists of a center electronics cabinet flanked by matching display units. On the next few pages, we explain how to build the electronics cabinet. Refer to the directions on page 21 to construct the display units.*

Begin with the cabinet sides

1. To form the cabinet's two sides (A), use the dimensions on the Exploded View Drawing, page 17, to mark the dado locations across the full width of a 4×8′ sheet of oak plywood. See the Cutting Diagram, page 17, for layout reference. (The top dado becomes a rabbet later when you trim the plywood panel to length.) Double-check your marked dado locations—4×8′ sheets of oak plywood aren't cheap. *continued*

MODULAR ENTERTAINMENT CENTER
continued

A

Mark all dado locations first. Then position and clamp a straightedge in place, and use it as a guide to rout the ¾"-wide dadoes.

2. Chuck a ¾" straight bit into your router. Using a board as a straightedge, rout ¾" dadoes ¼" deep across the plywood panel as shown in photo A *above*. (Routing the dadoes in the large panel and then cutting the sides from the panel ensures perfectly aligned dadoes.)

3. Fit your portable circular saw with a plywood-cutting blade. Cut along the top shoulder of the top dado to trim the 8' plywood sheet to 83" long (see the drawing *below* for the location of the cut).

4. Rip two 21¼"-wide sides (A) from each plywood panel.

5. Cut a ¼" rabbet ½" deep along the *back inside* edge of each cabinet side. Mark the location first; it's easy to rout along the wrong edge.

6. Rip two ¼"-thick by 22"-long strips (B) from the edge of a ¾"-thick oak board. With the edges flush, glue and tape a strip to the bottom end of each side panel (we used masking tape since most clamps aren't long enough). Later, remove the tape, and trim the strip ends flush with the cabinet sides. Sand the strip edges flush with the face of the cabinet sides. Sand a slight round-over along each strip's bottom edge.

Cut the top, bottom, and fixed shelves

1. Rip two 21"-wide panels from a 4×8' sheet of oak-veneer plywood.

2. Cut the top, bottom, and three fixed shelves (C) to length (29") from the two strips.

3. Mark the location of the wiring and cooling notch along the back edge of the top shelf (see the Exploded View Drawing, *opposite*). Cut the notch to size.
continued

Bill of Materials				
Part	Finished Size*		Mat.	Qty.
	T	W	L		
Basic Cabinet					
A* side	¾"	21¼"	83"	OP	2
B* strip	¾"	¼"	21¼"	O	2
C shelf	¾"	21"	29"	OP	5
D back	¼"	29½"	80¾"	OP	1
Face Frame					
E rail	¾"	3"	30⅛"	O	2
F stile	¾"	1⁹⁄₁₆"	77"	O	2
G shelf facing	¾"	1½"	27"	O	3
Upper and Lower Doors					
H panel	¾"	12⁹⁄₁₆"	11¼"	OP	2
I* banding	¾"	⅜"	11¼"	O	4
J* banding	¾"	⅜"	13⁵⁄₁₆"	O	8
K panel	¾"	12⁹⁄₁₆"	24"	OP	2
L* banding	¾"	⅜"	24"	O	4
Drawer					
M front	½"	5⅜"	25½"	O	1
N side	½"	5⅜"	20"	O	2
O back	½"	4⅞"	25½"	O	1
P bottom	¼"	15¾"	25½"	OP	1
Q face	¾"	5"	26"	OP	1
R* banding	¾"	⅜"	5"	O	2
S* banding	¾"	⅜"	26¾"	O	2
T filler block	¾"	6¾"	21"	OP	2
Adjustable Shelf					
U shelf	¾"	20"	28¼"	OP	1
V facing	¾"	1½"	28¼"	O	1
Display Cabinet Doors					
W panel	¾"	12⁹⁄₁₆"	18¾"	OP	2
X banding	¾"	⅜"	18¾"	O	4
Y banding	¾"	⅜"	13⁵⁄₁₆"	O	4

*Parts marked with an * are cut larger initially, then trimmed to finished size. Please read the instructions before cutting.

Material Key: O—oak, OP—oak plywood.
Supplies: #17×1" brads, #8×1¼" flathead wood screws, #8×1" flathead wood screws, #17×¾" brads, stain, finish.

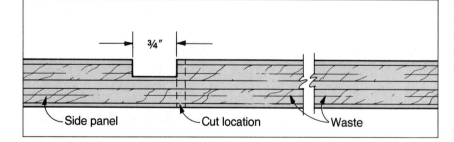

¾"

Side panel — Cut location — Waste

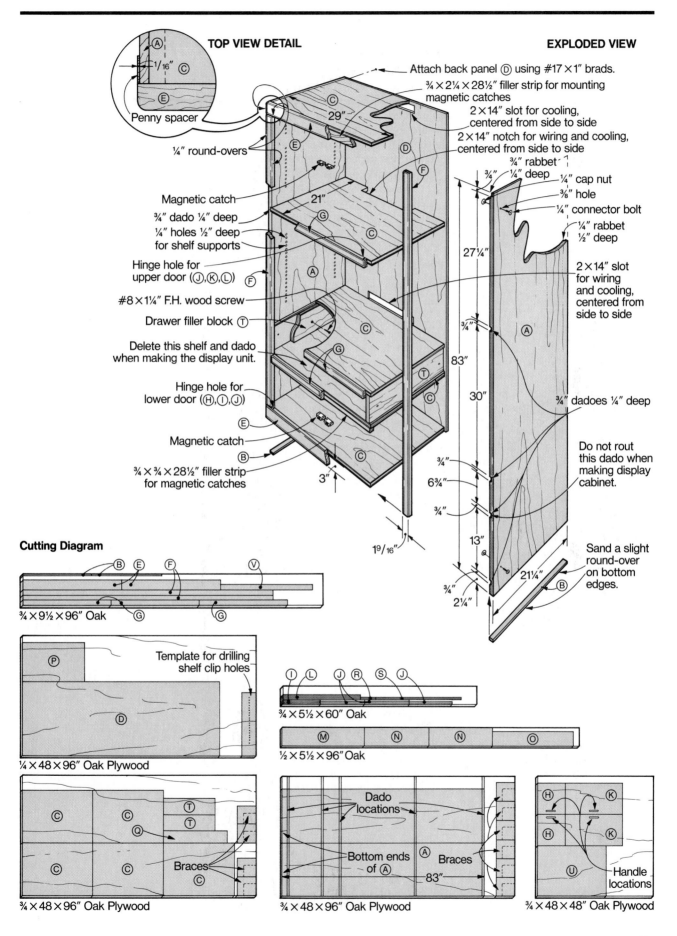

TOP VIEW DETAIL

Ⓐ

1/16" Ⓒ

Ⓔ

Penny spacer

¼" round-overs

Magnetic catch

¾" dado ¼" deep

¼" holes ½" deep
for shelf supports

Hinge hole for
upper door (Ⓙ,Ⓚ,Ⓛ)

#8 × 1¼" F.H. wood screw

Drawer filler block Ⓣ

Delete this shelf and dado
when making the display unit.

Hinge hole for
lower door (Ⓗ,Ⓘ,Ⓙ)

Magnetic catch

¾ × ¾ × 28½" filler strip
for magnetic catches

3"

EXPLODED VIEW

Attach back panel Ⓓ using #17 × 1" brads.

¾ × 2¼ × 28½" filler strip for mounting
magnetic catches

2 × 14" slot for cooling,
centered from side to side

2 × 14" notch for wiring and cooling,
centered from side to side

¾" rabbet
¼" deep

¾"   ¼" cap nut

⅜" hole

¼" connector bolt

¼" rabbet
½" deep

2 × 14" slot
for wiring
and cooling,
centered from
side to side

¾"

¾" dadoes ¼" deep

Do not rout
this dado when
making display
cabinet.

Sand a slight
round-over
on bottom
edges.

29"

21"

Ⓐ

Ⓒ

Ⓒ

Ⓖ

Ⓖ

Ⓣ

83"

27¼"

30"

¾"

6¾"

¾"

13"

¾"

2¼"

21¼"

Ⓑ

1⁹⁄₁₆"

Cutting Diagram

Ⓑ Ⓔ   Ⓕ   Ⓥ

Ⓖ   Ⓖ

¾ × 9½ × 96" Oak

Ⓟ

Template for drilling
shelf clip holes

Ⓓ

¼ × 48 × 96" Oak Plywood

Ⓘ Ⓛ   Ⓙ Ⓡ   Ⓢ   Ⓙ

¾ × 5½ × 60" Oak

Ⓜ   Ⓝ   Ⓝ   Ⓞ

½ × 5½ × 96" Oak

Ⓒ   Ⓒ   Ⓣ
          Ⓠ   Ⓣ

Ⓒ   Ⓒ
              Ⓒ

Braces

¾ × 48 × 96" Oak Plywood

Dado
locations

Bottom ends
of Ⓐ

Ⓐ   Braces

83"

¾ × 48 × 96" Oak Plywood

Ⓗ   Ⓚ

Ⓗ   Ⓚ

Ⓤ

Handle
locations

¾ × 48 × 48" Oak Plywood

MODULAR ENTERTAINMENT CENTER
continued

Assemble the cabinet

1. Cut 10 braces to the size shown on the Brace Drawing, *below,* and as laid out on the Cutting Diagram, page 17.

2. Glue and clamp the bottom (C) in the lowest dado of a side panel (A) as shown in

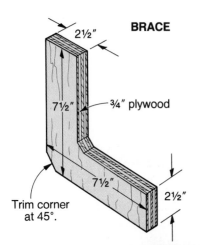

BRACE

2½"

7½" — ¾" plywood

7½"

2½"

Trim corner at 45°.

Clamp the bottom, fixed, and top shelves into the dadoes, using scrap braces to keep them square until the glue dries.

photo B *above.* Use two braces for stability and to ensure squareness. Repeat the process to glue the top in the rabbet at the opposite end of the side panel. Be sure that the *back edges* of the top and bottom are flush with the *inside edges* of the rabbet. Wipe off any glue squeeze-out with a

damp cloth. After the glue dries, remove the braces. With a helper, turn the assembly over, and repeat the process to glue and clamp the second side panel (A) to the assembly; check for square.

3. Measure the opening, and cut the cabinet back (D) to size from ¼" oak plywood. Hold the back in place with masking tape, and mark the location of the two cooling slots shown on the Exploded View Drawing, page 17. Remove the back from the cabinet. Drill a blade start hole and cut the slots to size. Set the back aside for now—to avoid stain marks across the grain, stain it later, then nail in place.

Put on the face frame

1. Rip and crosscut the oak face-frame top and bottom rails (E) to size—the width of the cabinet plus ⅛" to allow for a 1/16" overhang beyond each side panel.

2. Rout ¼" round-overs along the front face of each rail where shown on the Exploded View Drawing. Sand the routed rails smooth (we used a palm sander). Drill 5/16" holes ⅜" deep in the rails (E) for the plastic bushings where shown on the Pivot Hinge Drawing, *opposite.* Glue and clamp the rails to the cabinet with a 1/16" overhang on each of the ends.

3. Measure the distance between the top and bottom rails (E), and cut the face-frame stiles (F) to size. Rout ¼" round-overs along the front face of each stile. Sand the routed ends.

4. As shown in photo C, *above right,* glue and clamp the oak stiles to the cabinet front, using a

Using a penny as a spacer for an even overhang, glue and clamp the stiles to the cabinet front.

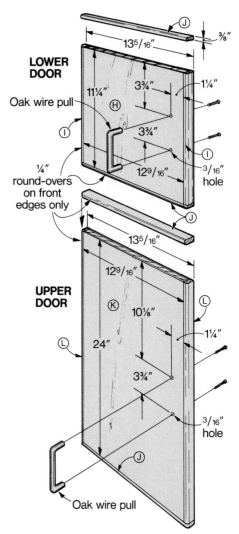

LOWER DOOR

13⁵/₁₆"

⅜"

11¼"

3¾"

1¼"

Oak wire pull

(H)

(I)

3¾"

¼" round-overs on front edges only

12⁹/₁₆"

³/₁₆" hole

(J)

(J)

UPPER DOOR

13⁵/₁₆"

12⁹/₁₆"

10⅛"

(K)

(L)

(L)

24"

1¼"

3¾"

³/₁₆" hole

(J)

Oak wire pull

penny as a spacer. (We applied masking tape to the adjoining areas to protect the plywood from excess glue.) Allow the glue to dry, and then remove the clamps and tape.

5. Turn the cabinet over so it's resting on its face. Apply masking tape to the areas next to the dadoes. Brush glue in the dadoes in the cabinet sides. Then slide the three fixed shelves (C) into place, and use the braces to keep the shelves square while the glue dries.

6. Measure the distance between the stiles (F), and cut the shelf facing (G) to length. Rout ¼" round-overs along the front of each. Drill ⁵⁄₁₆" holes ⅜" deep in the facing (G) for the plastic bushings where shown on the Pivot Hinge Drawing. Glue and clamp a facing strip to the front of each of the three shelves.

Build and hang the doors

1. Referring to the Upper and Lower Door drawings, *opposite, lower right,* cut the lower door panels (H) to size. To match the grain from door to door, note and mark the approximate location of the oak wire pulls on each door where shown on the Cutting Diagram, page 17.

2. Rip four ⅜"-wide by 12"-long banding strips (I) from the edge of ¾" stock. Glue and clamp them to the sides of both door panels. Later, trim the ends of the strips flush with the top and bottom of the door panels. Repeat this process to cut and adhere the banding strips (J) to the top and bottom of each door. Sand the doors smooth.

3. Repeat steps 1 and 2 *above* to build the upper doors (J, K, L).

4. Using the dimensions on the door drawings, carefully mark the centerpoints on each door for the holes you'll use to fasten the oak wire pulls. Drill the holes to size.

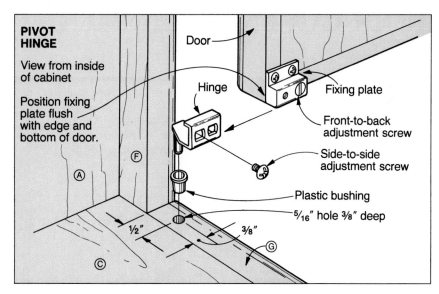

5. Rout ¼" round-overs along the front face of each door.

6. Using the Pivot Hinge Drawing *above* for reference, fasten a fixing plate flush with the top and bottom inside corners of each cabinet door. (See the Buying Guide on page 21 for our hardware source.)

7. Insert a bushing into each hinge hole. Fit a hinge into each bushing, slide the fixing plates (attached to the door) into the hinges, and then thread the side-to-side adjustment screw through the hinge and into the fixing plate. Position the two adjustment screws as necessary for a good fit of the doors.

8. Cut the filler strips (dimensioned on the Exploded View Drawing, page 17) to size—these support the magnetic catches. Glue and clamp the oak strips to the back of the top rail (E) and to the back of the bottom shelf facing (G) where shown on the Exploded View Drawing. Attach magnetic catches to the filler strips, and fasten the strike plates to the back of the doors. Remove the doors from the cabinet. Now remove the fixing plates, strikes, and hinges (you'll reattach them after finishing).

Fashion the videotape drawer

1. Rip and crosscut the drawer front (M), sides (N), back (O), and bottom (P) to the sizes listed in the Bill of Materials, page 16.

2. Cut or rout a ½" rabbet ¼" deep across the front of each drawer side. (See the Drawer Drawing, page 20, for reference.) Now cut a ½" dado ¼" deep 4" from the back of each drawer side. Finally, cut a ¼" groove ¼" deep ¼" from the bottom edge into the drawer sides (N) and drawer front (M). Dry-clamp the pieces to check the fit.

3. Glue and clamp the drawer together, checking for square. Do not glue the bottom (P) in the ¼" groove; instead, secure it to the back (O) with ¾" brads.

4. Cut the drawer face (Q) to size. Now cut the banding strips (R, S) to size plus 1" in length. Glue and clamp the banding strips (R) to the ends of the drawer face. When dry, trim off the excess. Repeat the process to add the top and bottom banding strips (S). Rout ¼" round-overs along the front face of the banded drawer face. *continued*

MODULAR ENTERTAINMENT CENTER
continued

Install the drawer

1. Cut the filler blocks (T) to size. Drill and countersink a pair of shank holes in each block, and screw the blocks to the inside of the drawer opening where shown on the Exploded View Drawing, page 17.

2. Following the directions supplied with the drawer slides, attach the slides to the drawer sides and the filler blocks. Install the drawer.

3. Place a piece of double-faced tape on the front face of the drawer front (M). Then position the banded drawer face (Q, R, S), centered from side to side and top to bottom. (We taped a nickel to each end and two nickels on the bottom edge to help center the drawer face in the opening and against the drawer front.) When correctly positioned, press firmly against the taped drawer face.

4. Remove the drawer and taped-on face, and clamp the drawer face to the drawer. Drill two holes through the drawer face and drawer front for the wire pull screws (see the Drawer Drawing, *above right*, for reference). From inside the drawer, drill and countersink four holes through the drawer front and just into the back of the drawer face. Drill a $7/64''$ pilot hole $\frac{1}{2}''$ deep into the back side of the drawer face. In the next step, you'll fasten the drawer face to the drawer front.

5. Pry the drawer face from the drawer front and remove the tape. Enlarge the two $5/32''$ holes for the wire pull in the drawer front (M) to $\frac{1}{2}''$. Screw the drawer face to the drawer front with wood screws.

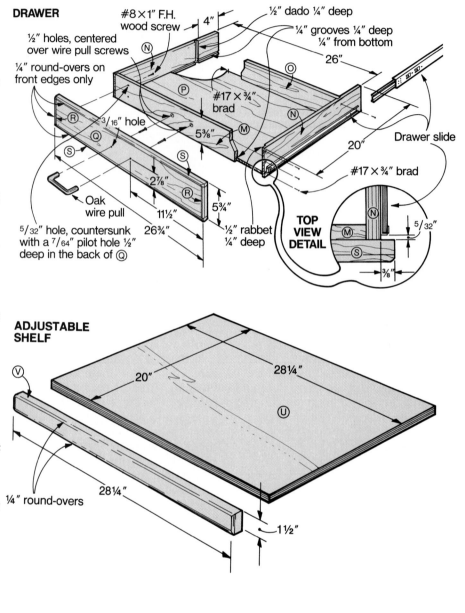

DRAWER

#8×1" F.H. wood screw

$\frac{1}{2}''$ holes, centered over wire pull screws

$\frac{1}{4}''$ round-overs on front edges only

$\frac{1}{2}''$ dado $\frac{1}{4}''$ deep

$\frac{1}{4}''$ grooves $\frac{1}{4}''$ deep $\frac{1}{4}''$ from bottom

26"

4"

N

O

P

#17 × $\frac{3}{4}''$ brad

M

N

$3/16''$ hole

R

Q

S

5$\frac{3}{8}''$

20"

Drawer slide

#17 × $\frac{3}{4}''$ brad

Oak wire pull

S

2$\frac{7}{8}''$

R

11$\frac{1}{2}''$

5$\frac{3}{4}''$

$5/32''$ hole, countersunk with a $7/64''$ pilot hole $\frac{1}{2}''$ deep in the back of Q

26$\frac{3}{4}''$

$\frac{1}{2}''$ rabbet $\frac{1}{4}''$ deep

TOP VIEW DETAIL

N

$5/32$

M

S

$\frac{3}{8}''$

ADJUSTABLE SHELF

V

20"

28$\frac{1}{4}''$

U

$\frac{1}{4}''$ round-overs

28$\frac{1}{4}''$

1$\frac{1}{2}''$

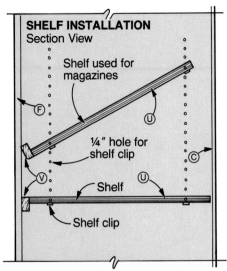

SHELF INSTALLATION
Section View

Shelf used for magazines

F

U

¼" hole for shelf clip

C

V

Shelf

U

Shelf clip

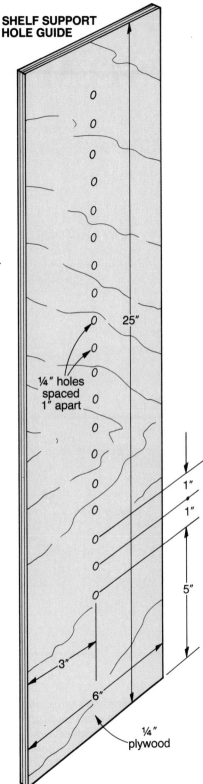

SHELF SUPPORT HOLE GUIDE

25"

¼" holes spaced 1" apart

1"

1"

5"

3"

6"

¼" plywood

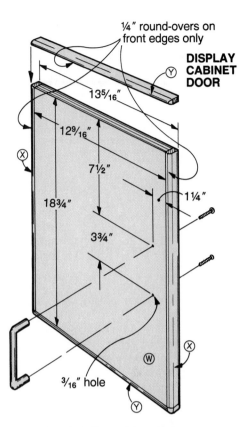

¼" round-overs on front edges only

DISPLAY CABINET DOOR

Y

13⁵⁄₁₆"

12⁹⁄₁₆"

X

7½"

1¼"

18¾"

3¾"

³⁄₁₆" hole

W

X

Y

Make the adjustable shelf and complete the assembly

1. Referring to the Adjustable Shelf Drawing, *opposite, bottom,* cut the shelf (U) and the front facing strip (V) to size. Rout a ¼" round-over along the front face of the strip.

2. Glue and clamp the facing strip to the front of the shelf. The top edge of the strip sits flush with the top face of the shelf.

3. To drill the shelf-clip holes for the adjustable shelf, start by making a hole guide like the one shown on the Shelf Support Hole Guide Drawing at *right.* Position the guide flush with the back edge of the rabbet in the cabinet side, and drill ¼" holes. (We used a stop on our drill bit to keep from drilling through the cabinet side.) Keeping the same end down, move the guide from the back to the front along each side and drill the holes.

4. If you plan to build more than one cabinet, we recommend using joint-connector bolts and cap nuts to hold a set of cabinets together. (See the Buying Guide for our source, and the Exploded View Drawing, page 17, for reference.)

5. Sand smooth the cabinet, cabinet back, doors, adjustable shelf, and drawer. Apply the stain and finish. Finally, glue and nail the back into the rabbet in the back of the cabinet. Attach the hardware, install the drawer, and hang the doors.

Build a display cabinet or two

The display cabinet varies from the electronics cabinet in a few ways. First, don't cut the dadoes or add the fixed shelf shown second from the bottom on the Exploded View Drawing. Also, delete the drawer and lower doors. Instead, build the display cabinet doors shown *above.* To display magazines, turn an adjustable shelf upside down and angle it as shown on the Shelf Install-ation Drawing *above, far left.*

Buying Guide
• **Hardware.** Brass-plated shelf clips, catalog no. 33894. Full-extension 18" drawer slide, catalog no. 32490. Magnetic catch, catalog no. 26559. Pivot hinge and fixing plate, catalog no. 30007. Oak wire pull, catalog no. 30098. Joint-connector bolt, catalog no. 31831. Cap nut, catalog no. 31815. For current prices, contact The Woodworkers' Store, 21801 Industrial Blvd., Rogers, MN 55374-9514. Or call 612/428-2199.

ARCHED-TOP SHELVING SYSTEM

L ooking for an attractive way to integrate your audio and video equipment and display your prized collectibles? If so, consider our modular wall system; it's easy to build, assemble, and add onto. The four-unit system shown here occupies almost 12 feet of wall space. But the project looks just as good if you build only one or two of the 34"-wide units.

Note: The instructions explain how to make the components for a single unit (two arches, one base, one back brace, one oak veneer plywood shelf, and one oak-framed glass shelf). The Bill of Materials, page 24, gives the number of pieces needed for a single unit. To make a second unit, you simply make one

additional arch, back brace, and base. If you're making more than one unit, we suggest you cut all identical pieces at the same time to ensure uniformity.

To build the wine rack and record rack that we've incorporated into our wall system, please refer to page 29.

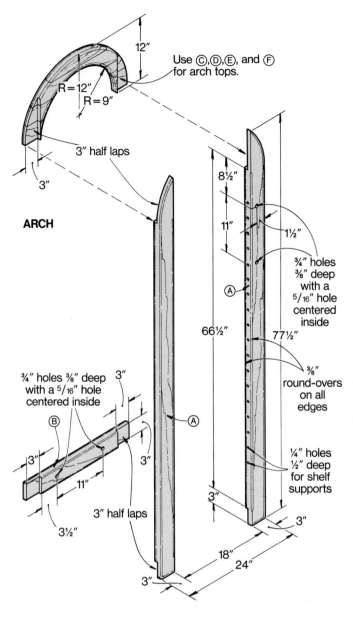

12"

Use ⓒ,ⓓ,ⓔ, and ⓕ
for arch tops.

R=12"
R=9"

3" half laps

3"

ARCH

¾" holes ⅜" deep
with a ⁵/₁₆" hole
centered inside

ⓑ

3"

3"

11"

3" half laps

3½"

8½"

11"

1½"

ⓐ

66½"

77½"

3"

18"

24"

3"

¾" holes
⅜" deep
with a
⁵/₁₆" hole
centered
inside

⅜"
round-overs
on all
edges

¼" holes
½" deep
for shelf
supports

FORMING THE ARCH TOP

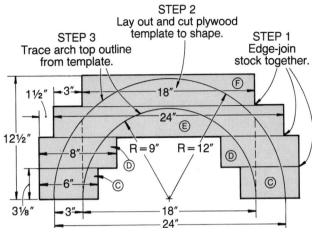

STEP 2
Lay out and cut plywood
template to shape.

STEP 3
Trace arch top outline
from template.

STEP 1
Edge-join
stock together.

1½" 3"

12½"

3⅛"

8"

6"

3"

18"

24"

ⓕ

18"

24"

ⓔ

R = 9"   R = 12"

ⓓ

ⓒ

ⓓ

ⓒ

A

Mark the arch top outline with the template.

Start with the arches

1. Cut the uprights (A) to size plus 2″ in length. Cut the lower cross members (B) and the arch top pieces (C, D, E, F) to size.

2. Edge-join a pair of arch top blanks as shown on the Forming the Arch Top Drawing, *upper right*. (We glued and clamped the Cs to the Ds and the Es to the Fs, then we joined the two C–D laminations to each E–F to make two arch top blanks.)

3. To make a template for marking the arch tops, first cut a piece of plywood to 13×25″.

Then, using the radii given on the Forming the Arch Top Drawing, lay out an arch top on the plywood. Cut the plywood template to shape, and sand the cut edges smooth.

4. Scrape the excess glue off the laminated blank, lay the template onto it, and trace the outline of the arch top as shown in photo A *above*.

5. Using a square, mark the inside edge of each half-lap joint (18″ apart) on each arch top lamination as shown on the sketch at *right*. *continued*

**MARKING
THE DADO
LOCATIONS**

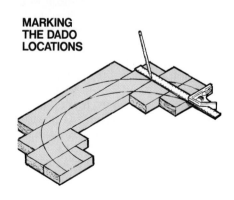

ARCHED-TOP SHELVING SYSTEM
continued

Note: *When cutting the half-lap joints on the ends of the arch tops, lower cross members, and uprights, be sure to cut the joints on the* same *side of each piece.*

6. To cut the arch half laps, set your saw so it cuts half the thickness of your material. Working from either end of the blank, cut away the material up to the mark you just made (see photo B *below*). Repeat this

B

Dado the arch top half-lap joints.

process at each end of each blank. Using a bandsaw, cut the arch tops to shape, cutting slightly *outside* the marked outlines (you'll need to re-mark the portion of the arch outline that you will lose when you cut the half-lap joints).

7. Cut a 3″ half-lap joint on both ends of the lower cross member (B) and the *bottom* end of each upright where shown on the Arch Drawing, page 23. To mark the location of the half lap at the *top* of each upright, measure up 66½″ from the *top* edge of the half lap joint you cut in each upright, and mark a line across the uprights at that point. Cut to the marked line to form the half laps.

8. Glue and clamp each arch together, checking for square. After the glue dries, remove the

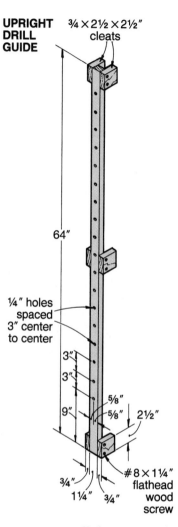

UPRIGHT DRILL GUIDE

¾ × 2½ × 2½″ cleats

64″

¼″ holes spaced 3″ center to center

3″
3″
9″
5⁄8″
5⁄8″
2½″

¾″
1¼″
¾″

#8 × 1¼″ flathead wood screw

clamps, scrape off the excess glue, and trim the uprights to match the curvature of the arch top.

9. Sand the arch tops to finished size (we sanded the inside curve with a drum sander and the outside with a belt sander). Sand the arches smooth, then rout a ⅜″ round-over along all edges.

10. To drill the shelf-support holes in the uprights, start by building the Upright Drill Guide shown *above*. **continued**

Bill of Materials				
Part	Finished Size*		Mat.	Qty.
	T	W	L		
Two Arches					
A* upright	1¼″	3″	77½″	O	4
B lower member	1¼″	3″	24″	O	2
C top	1¼″	3⅛″	6″	O	4
D top	1¼″	3⅛″	8″	O	4
E top	1¼″	3⅛″	24″	O	2
F top	1¼″	3⅛″	18″	O	2
One Back Brace and Base					
G lateral piece	1¼″	3″	31½″	O	4
H end	1¼″	3″	18¼″	O	4
I base shelf	¾″	18″	30″	OP	1
J trim	¾″	¾″	31½″	O	2
K trim	¾″	¾″	18″	O	2
One Oak Veneer Shelf					
L shelf	¾″	15½″	31¾″	OP	1
M trim	¾″	1⅛″	34″	O	2
N trim	¾″	1⅛″	15½″	O	2
One Oak-Framed Glass Shelf					
O frame	¾″	1¾″	34″	O	2
P frame	¾″	1¾″	17¾″	O	2

*Part marked with an * is cut larger initially, then trimmed to finished size. Please read the instructions before cutting.

Material Key: O—oak, OP—oak plywood.
Supplies: ¼ × 1¾″ roundhead machine screws (for double joint), ¼ × 3″ roundhead machine screws (for triple joint, used when making more than one unit), ¼″ flat washers, #6 × ½″ flathead wood screws, #8 × 1¼″ flathead wood screws, stain, polyurethane, ¼″ smoked glass for shelves.

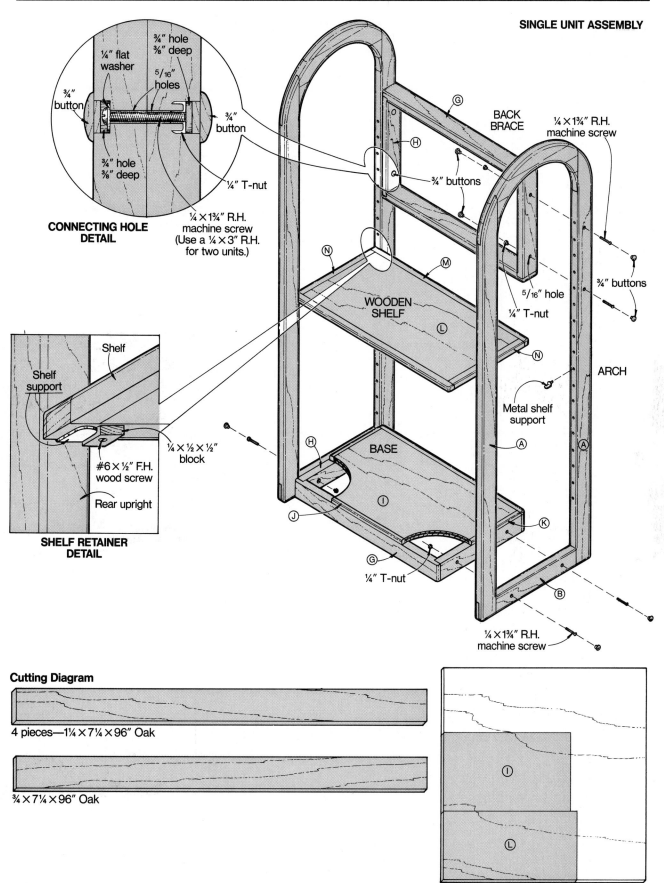

CONNECTING HOLE DETAIL

¼" flat washer
¾" hole ⅜" deep
5/16" holes
¾" button
¾" button
¾" hole ⅜" deep
¼" T-nut
¼ × 1¾" R.H. machine screw (Use a ¼ × 3" R.H. for two units.)

SHELF RETAINER DETAIL

Shelf
Shelf support
¼ × ½ × ½" block
#6 × ½" F.H. wood screw
Rear upright

BACK BRACE
¼ × 1¾" R.H. machine screw
¾" buttons
5/16" hole
¼" T-nut
¾" buttons

WOODEN SHELF

Metal shelf support

ARCH

BASE

¼" T-nut

¼ × 1¾" R.H. machine screw

Cutting Diagram

4 pieces—1¼ × 7¼ × 96" Oak

¾ × 7¼ × 96" Oak

¾ × 48 × 48" Oak Plywood

25

ARCHED-TOP SHELVING SYSTEM
continued

11. Position the drill guide against an upright, and drill ¼″ holes ½″ deep, as shown *below.* (The drill guide ensures consistent spacing from one upright to the next and eliminates wobbly shelves later. This is nearly impossible to do by measuring and drilling the holes one at a time.)

USING THE UPRIGHT DRILL GUIDE

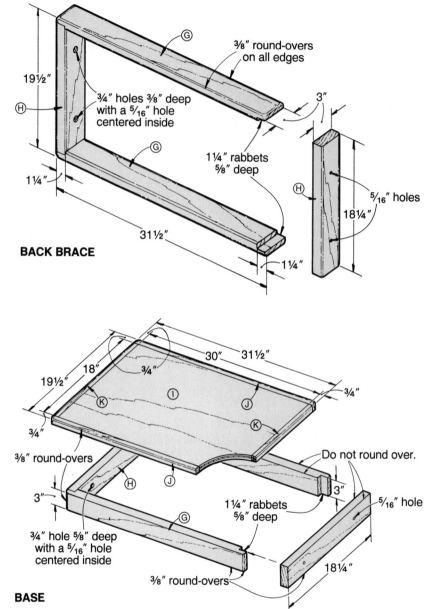

19½″

¾″ holes ⅜″ deep with a ⁵⁄₁₆″ hole centered inside

⅜″ round-overs on all edges

3″

H

1¼″ rabbets ⅝″ deep

H

⁵⁄₁₆″ holes

18¼″

1¼″

31½″

1¼″

BACK BRACE

30″   31½″

18″   ¾″

19½″

¾″

K   I   J   ¾″

K

⅜″ round-overs

Do not round over.

3″

H   J

G

1¼″ rabbets ⅝″ deep

3″

⁵⁄₁₆″ hole

¾″ hole ⅝″ deep with a ⁵⁄₁₆″ hole centered inside

⅜″ round-overs

18¼″

BASE

Build the back brace and the base

1. To make the back brace and frame for the base (they're identical in size), refer to the Back Brace Drawing, *top right,* and cut the lateral pieces (G) and the ends (H) to size. Cut a 1¼″ rabbet ⅝″ deep across each end of the laterals.

2. Glue and clamp the two frames together, checking for square. Later, scrape off the excess glue and sand.

3. Rout a ⅜″ round-over along all edges of the back brace. *Do not* rout the base just yet.

4. To make the base shelf (I), refer to the Base Drawing, *bottom right,* and rip then crosscut a

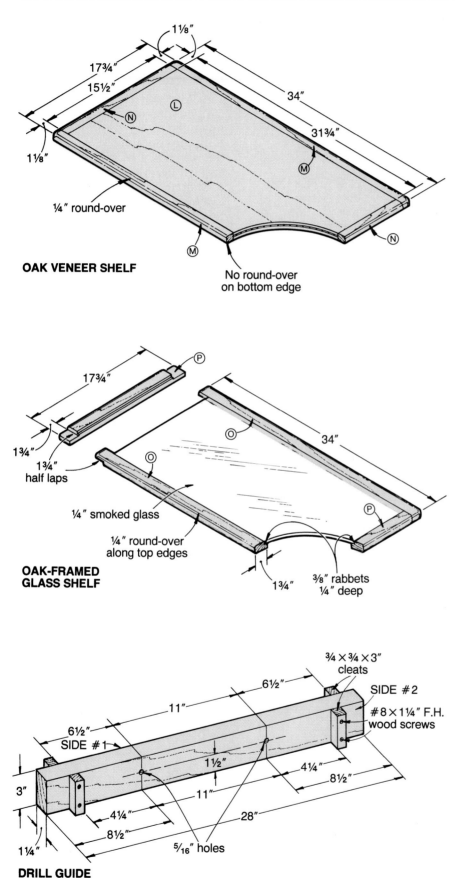

OAK VENEER SHELF

1⅛″
17¾″
15½″
34″
31¾″
1⅛″
¼″ round-over
No round-over on bottom edge

OAK-FRAMED GLASS SHELF

17¾″
1¾″
1¾″ half laps
¼″ smoked glass
¼″ round-over along top edges
34″
1¾″
⅜″ rabbets ¼″ deep

DRILL GUIDE

¾ × ¾ × 3″ cleats
6½″
11″
SIDE #2
6½″
SIDE #1
1½″
4¼″
8½″
11″
4¼″
28″
8½″
3″
1¼″
5/16″ holes
#8 × 1¼″ F.H. wood screws

piece of ¾″ oak veneer plywood to size. Cut the trim pieces (J, K) to size. Glue and clamp the trim pieces to the plywood. After the glue dries, remove the clamps, scrape off any excess glue, and sand the base shelf smooth. Glue and clamp the base shelf to the base, checking that all edges align flush and that the shelf is clamped firmly along the top edges of the base.

5. Sand the base smooth and rout a ⅜″ round-over along all top edges.

Make the shelves

Note: The wall unit shown has both oak veneer plywood shelves and an oak-framed glass variation. We'll show you how to build both types.

1. To make an *oak veneer shelf,* cut a piece of ¾″ oak veneer plywood (L) to 15½ × 31¾″, as shown on the Oak Veneer Shelf Drawing, *top left.*

2. Cut the trim pieces (M, N) to size. Glue and clamp the trim pieces to the edges of the plywood. Later, sand smooth and rout a ¼″ round-over on the top edges only. *Do not* rout the bottom edges.

3. To make an *oak-framed glass shelf,* refer to the Oak-Framed Glass Shelf Drawing, *center left,* and cut frame members (O, P) to size. Cut half-lap joints on the ends, and glue and clamp the pieces together, checking for square. Sand smooth, and rout a ⅜″ rabbet ¼″ deep on the top inside edge and a ¼″ round-over along the top outside edge. Using a chisel, square the rounded rabbeted corners. Have smoked glass cut to fit each shelf.

Drill the connecting holes and assemble the pieces

1. To drill matching holes in the arches, back brace, and base, make the drill guide shown at *bottom left.* *continued*

ARCHED-TOP SHELVING SYSTEM
continued

2. Position *Side 1* of the guide against a lower cross member (B), and drill a pair of 5/16" holes as shown on the sketch at *top right.* Repeat for each cross member.

3. Using *Side 2* of the drill guide, drill a pair of 5/16" holes through each end of each base and back brace as shown on the sketch at *center right.*

4. Remove both cleats from either side of the guide. Use the guide to drill a pair of 5/16" holes in each rear upright as shown on the sketch at *bottom right.*

5. Drill 3/4" holes 3/8" deep centered over the 5/16" holes on the inside of each back brace and base (we used a Forstner bit to accurately center the 3/4" holes directly over the 5/16" holes). Drill the same size holes in the rear upright and lower cross member of each arch.

Finish the pieces, then assemble

1. Finish-sand all the pieces now, before they are assembled. Finish as desired (we finished ours with a light reddish stain and several coats of polyurethane).

Note: For greatest ease, assemble your system with the front side down on the floor. Then, with helpers if the system is more than one unit long, raise it upright against the wall.

2. To assemble the pieces, start by positioning a base between two arch bottoms. Insert a 1/4" T-nut in each 3/4" hole on the inside face of each base end where shown on the Connecting Hole Detail accompanying the Single

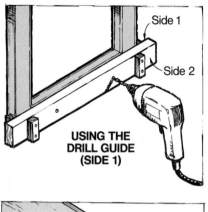

USING THE
DRILL GUIDE
(SIDE 1)

Side 1
Side 2

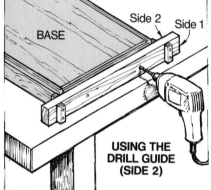

USING THE
DRILL GUIDE
(SIDE 2)

BASE
Side 2
Side 1

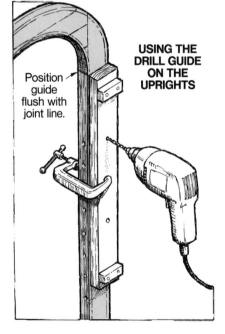

USING THE
DRILL GUIDE
ON THE
UPRIGHTS

Position guide flush with joint line.

Unit Assembly Drawing, page 25. (We misaligned a few of our 3/4" holes and had to grind the T-nuts to fit into both the 3/4" and 5/16" holes.) Slide a 1/4" machine screw and washer into each 3/4" hole in each arch bottom and thread the machine screw into the mating T-nut. Now repeat these procedures with the back brace. Tighten the screws. Later, insert 3/4" screw-hole buttons in the 3/4" holes to hide the screws and T-nuts.

3. To ensure that the shelves will stay put when you install them, cut two 1/4 × 1/2 × 1/2" retainers for each shelf. Insert four shelf supports in the uprights at the same level, and position a shelf on them. Mark the position of the two shelf supports along the bottom back edge of each shelf. Drill and countersink a hole in each retainer, and screw in place where shown on the Shelf Retainer Detail accompanying the Single Unit Assembly Drawing.

Buying Guide
• **Hardware.** T-nuts, 1/4-20, catalog no. 26054 for a package of 10. Oak screw-hole buttons, catalog no. 20669 for a package of 10. Brass-finish shelf supports, catalog no. 33894 for a package of 20. For information on current prices, contact The Woodworkers' Store, 21801 Industrial Blvd., Rogers, MN 55374-9514. Or call 612/428-2199.

Record Rack

EXPLODED VIEW

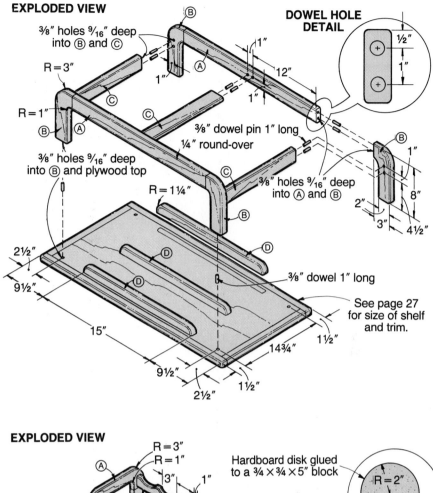

³⁄₈" holes ⁹⁄₁₆" deep into Ⓑ and Ⓒ

R = 3"

R = 1"

³⁄₈" holes ⁹⁄₁₆" deep into Ⓑ and plywood top

R = 1¼"

Ⓐ

Ⓑ

Ⓒ

1"

12"

1"

2½"

9½"

15"

9½"

2½"

1½"

14¾"

1½"

³⁄₈" dowel pin 1" long
¼" round-over

³⁄₈" holes ⁹⁄₁₆" deep into Ⓐ and Ⓑ

Ⓓ

³⁄₈" dowel 1" long

See page 27 for size of shelf and trim.

1"

8"

2"

3"

4½"

DOWEL HOLE DETAIL

½"

1"

Bill of Materials

Part	Finished Size			Mat.	Qty.
	T	W	L		
A rail	¾"	2"	25"	O	2
B end	¾"	3"	8"	O	4
C cross member	¾"	2"	14"	O	3
D stop	¾"	1¼"	15"	O	3

Material Key: O—oak.
Supplies: ³⁄₈" dowel stock, stain, finish.

Wine and Stemware Rack

EXPLODED VIEW

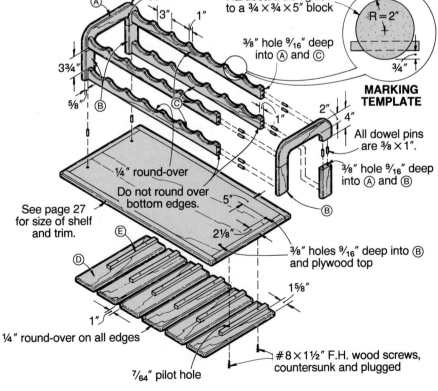

R = 3"
R = 1"

3"

1"

3¾"

5⁄₈"

Ⓐ

Ⓑ

Ⓒ

Hardboard disk glued to a ¾ × ¾ × 5" block

³⁄₈" hole ⁹⁄₁₆" deep into Ⓐ and Ⓒ

R = 2"

¾"

MARKING TEMPLATE

2"

4"

All dowel pins are ³⁄₈ × 1".

³⁄₈" hole ⁹⁄₁₆" deep into Ⓐ and Ⓑ

Ⓑ

¼" round-over
Do not round over bottom edges.

See page 27 for size of shelf and trim.

1"

5"

2⅛"

1⁵⁄₈"

³⁄₈" holes ⁹⁄₁₆" deep into Ⓑ and plywood top

Ⓔ

Ⓓ

¼" round-over on all edges

⁷⁄₆₄" pilot hole

#8 × 1½" F.H. wood screws, countersunk and plugged

Bill of Materials

Part	Finished Size			Mat.	Qty.
	T	W	L		
A end top	¾"	4"	10"	O	2
B end bottom	¾"	2"	5½"	O	4
C bottle rack	¾"	2"	29"	O	4
D stemware rack	¾"	4"	16"	O	6
E spacer	½"	¾"	10½"	O	6

Material Key: O—oak.
Supplies: #8 × 1½" flathead wood screws, ³⁄₈" dowel stock, stain, finish.

CHERRY CURIO CABINET

At first glance, our curio cabinet may seem like a major undertaking. But, if you'll take a good look at the drawings, you'll notice the entire project consists of just four subassemblies that form identical top and bottom cabinets. Come on; give this project a try. We know that you'll be pleased with the fine-furniture results.

Start with the four side frames

Note: For ease in construction, the side frames for the top and bottom cabinets match except for the rail placement. For a well-balanced design, we placed the wider rails (C) on the bottom of the bottom frames and along the top edge of the top frames. Study the drawings carefully before beginning construction of the side frames.

1. Referring to the Side Frames Drawing, *opposite, top,* cut the side-frame stiles (A, B) and rails (C, D) to the sizes listed in the Bill of Materials, page 33.

2. Clamp each frame together in the configurations shown on the Side Frames Drawing. Make marks for a pair of dowel holes at each glue joint. Remove the clamps. Using a doweling jig for alignment, drill ⅜" holes 1¾₁₆" deep at each mark.

Note: When working with cherry, immediately remove all excess glue to prevent light-colored marks from appearing after staining. We wiped off all the glue squeeze-out with a damp cloth after clamping.

3. Glue, dowel, and clamp each side frame, checking for square.

4. Mark the centerpoints, and drill the ¼" shelf holes ⁵⁄₁₆" deep where dimensioned on the Side Frames Drawing. Sand the frames.

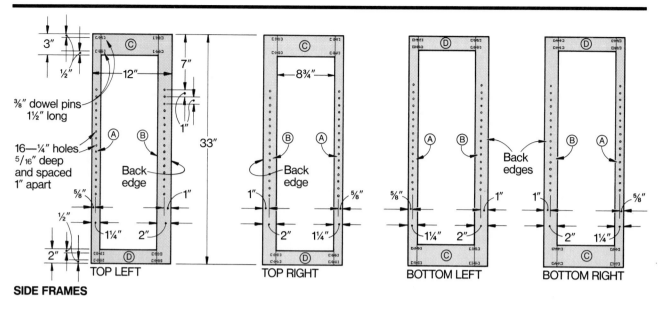

SIDE FRAMES

Labels on the side frames diagram: TOP LEFT, TOP RIGHT, BOTTOM LEFT, BOTTOM RIGHT

3"
½"
³⁄₈" dowel pins
1½" long
16—¼" holes
⁵⁄₁₆" deep
and spaced
1" apart
⅝"
½"
2"
12"
7"
1"
33"
8¾"
Back edge
Back edge
Back edges
⅝"
1"
1¼"
2"
½"
1¼"
2"
1"
1¼"
2"
⅝"
⅝"
2"
1¼"
1"

Build the three framed panels

1. Miter-cut the framed-panel fronts and backs (E) and the sides (F) to length from ¾"-thick stock 2" wide, as shown on the Framed Panel Drawing at *right*.

2. Using a dado blade or dado set mounted to your tablesaw, cut a ¼" rabbet ¼" deep along the top inside edge of each of the frame members.

3. Using band clamps, glue and clamp each frame together, checking for square. Later, remove the clamps, and sand each of the three frames smooth.

4. Measure the openings, and cut the insert panels (G) to fit from ¼" cherry plywood. Glue and clamp the insert panels into place.

5. Rout ¼" round-overs along the edges of the framed panels where noted on the Framed Panel Drawing. Sand each assembly smooth.

Attach the side frames

1. Using the Framed Panel Drawing for reference, mark centerpoints for the four screw locations on the top face of each framed panel. Drill the ⁵⁄₃₂" shank holes. Next, countersink the shank holes in the top and middle framed panels from the *top* side; then countersink the bottom framed panel from the *bottom* side.

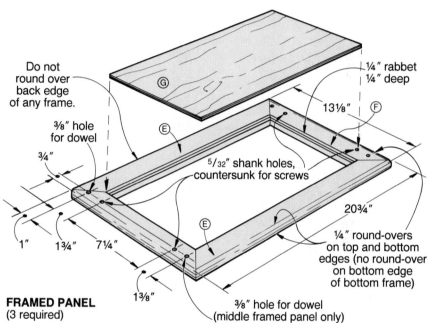

Do not round over back edge of any frame.

³⁄₈" hole for dowel
¾"
¼" rabbet ¼" deep
13⅛"
⁵⁄₃₂" shank holes, countersunk for screws
20¾"
¼" round-overs on top and bottom edges (no round-over on bottom edge of bottom frame)
1"
1¾"
7¼"
1⅜"
³⁄₈" hole for dowel (middle framed panel only)

FRAMED PANEL
(3 required)

2. Mark the four dowel-hole centerpoints on the top face of the middle framed panel (see the Framed Panel Drawing for locations). Drill the ³⁄₈" dowel holes where marked.

3. With the back edges flush, clamp the two bottom frames between the bottom and middle framed panels, checking for square. (See the Front View Detail accompanying the Cabinet Assembly Drawing, page 32, for frame location.) Using the previously drilled shank holes in the framed panels as guides, drill ⁷⁄₆₄" pilot holes ½" deep into the

side frames (see the Side View Detail, page 32, for reference). Now remove the clamps, and glue and screw the side frames between the framed panels.

4. Lay the bottom cabinet assembly on its back. Insert dowel centers into the ³⁄₈" dowel holes in the top face of the middle framed panel. Clamp the top side panels in position between the top framed assembly and bottom cabinet assembly to transfer the *continued*

31

CHERRY CURIO CABINET
continued

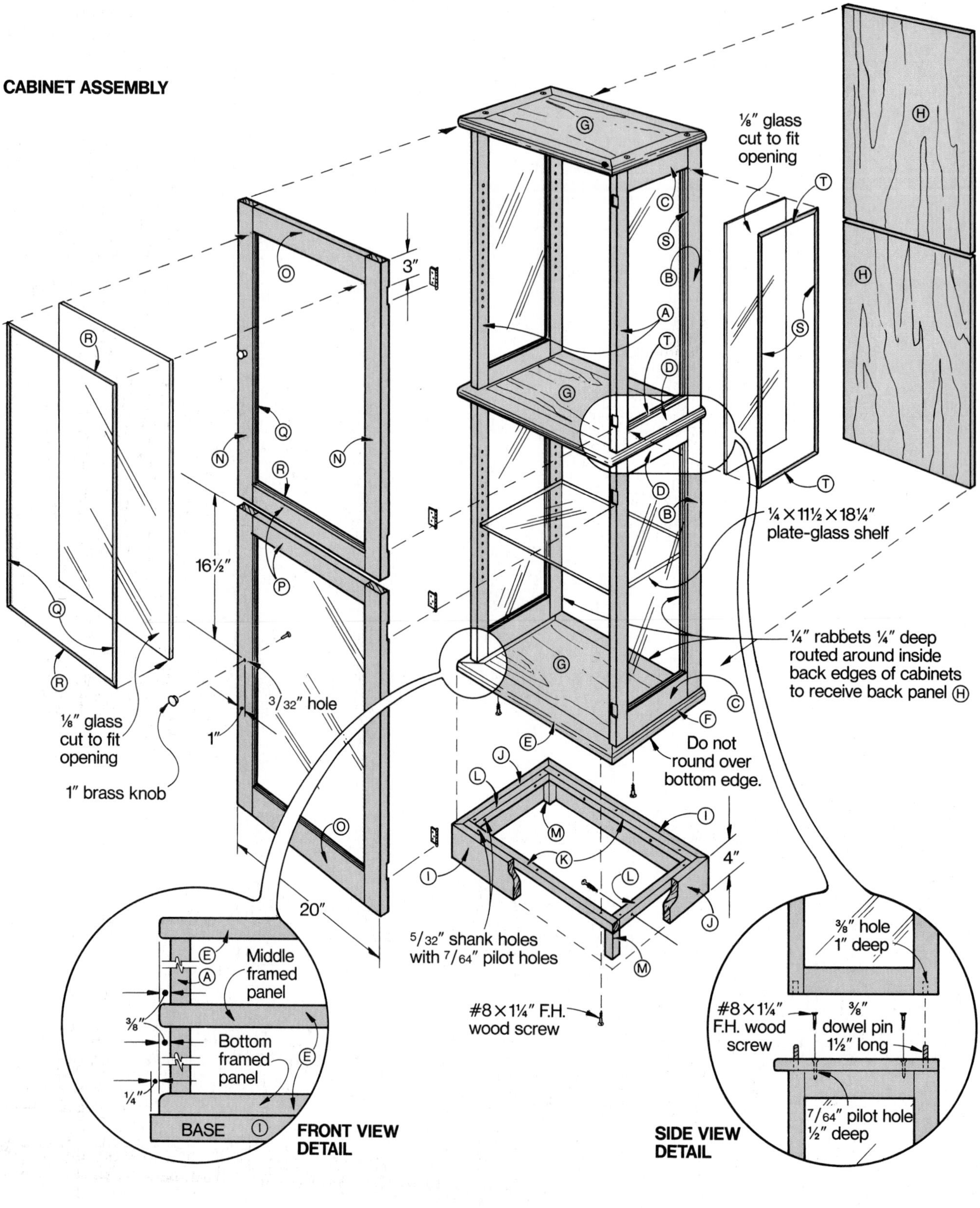

CABINET ASSEMBLY

¹⁄₈" glass cut to fit opening

3"

16½"

³⁄₃₂" hole

¹⁄₈" glass cut to fit opening

1" brass knob

1"

20"

¼ × 11½ × 18¼" plate-glass shelf

¼" rabbets ¼" deep routed around inside back edges of cabinets to receive back panel Ⓗ

Do not round over bottom edge.

⁵⁄₃₂" shank holes with ⁷⁄₆₄" pilot holes

#8 × 1¼" F.H. wood screw

FRONT VIEW DETAIL

Middle framed panel

Bottom framed panel

BASE

³⁄₈"

¼"

SIDE VIEW DETAIL

³⁄₈" hole 1" deep

#8 × 1¼" F.H. wood screw

³⁄₈" dowel pin 1½" long

⁷⁄₆₄" pilot hole ½" deep

dowel-hole centerpoints onto the bottom edge of the upper side frames. Using the previously drilled shank holes in the top framed assembly as guides, drill $^7\!/_{64}$" pilot holes $^1\!/_2$" deep into the top of the upper side frames.

5. Remove the top cabinet assembly, and drill the mating dowel holes in the bottom edge of the upper side frames where indented.

6. Install the dowel pins into the dowel holes in the middle framed panel. Next, glue the top cabinet to the bottom cabinet.

7. Carefully lay the cabinet facedown on a work surface covered with a blanket to prevent scratching the cabinet. Then rout a $^1\!/_4$" rabbet $^1\!/_4$" deep around the inside edge of the upper and lower cabinet assemblies for the $^1\!/_4$" plywood back panels (H). Finally, chisel the rounded corners square.

8. Cut the two back panels (H) to fit the rabbeted openings. Glue and brad the $^1\!/_4$" back panels into place (we used #18×$^1\!/_2$" brads).

Construct the base

1. Miter-cut the exterior base parts (I, J) to size. Now cut the base cleats (K, L), and glue blocks (M) to size. Drill and countersink screw holes into the cleats.

2. Glue and clamp the exterior parts together with a band clamp, checking for square. Then glue and screw the cleats into place flush with the top edge of the exterior base parts. Add the glue blocks, and sand the base smooth.

3. Set the cabinet upside down on a blanket. With the back edges flush, center the base (also upside down) from side to side on the bottom framed panel. Glue and screw the base to the lower framed panel.

Build the door frames

1. Rip and crosscut the door stiles (N) and rails (O, P) to size. Clamp each door frame together, and make marks for a pair of dowel holes at each joint line. Then, with a doweling jig, drill $^3\!/_8$" holes $^9\!/_{16}$" deep.

2. Glue, dowel, and clamp each door frame together, checking for square. Later, remove the clamps, and sand the door frames.

3. Place the cabinet on its back. Check the fit of the doors on the cabinet front. The sides of the doors should fit flush with the sides of the cabinet; plane the edges of the doors, if necessary. Also, be sure to leave a $^1\!/_{16}$" gap

between the top and bottom of the doors and the framed panels. (When fitting the doors, we marked one door as "upper" and the other as "lower" for ease in final assembly.)

Cut and install the glass stops

1. Cut nine pieces of $^3\!/_4$"-thick cherry to $1^1\!/_2$" wide by 36" long. Rout a $^1\!/_4$" round-over along all four edges of each piece.

2. As shown on the Forming the Glass Stops Drawing *below*, cut four *continued*

Bill of Materials

Part	Finished Size*			Mat.	Qty.
	T	W	L		
Four Side Frames					
A stile	$^3\!/_4$"	$1^1\!/_4$"	33"	C	4
B stile	$^3\!/_4$"	2"	33"	C	4
C rail	$^3\!/_4$"	3"	$8^3\!/_4$"	C	4
D rail	$^3\!/_4$"	2"	$8^3\!/_4$"	C	4
Three Framed Panels					
E front/ back	$^3\!/_4$"	2"	$20^3\!/_4$"	C	6
F side	$^3\!/_4$"	2"	$13^1\!/_8$"	C	6
G insert panel	$^1\!/_4$"	$9^5\!/_8$"	$17^1\!/_4$"	CP	3
Two Back Panels					
H back panel	$^1\!/_4$"	19"	$33^1\!/_2$"	CP	2
Base					
I exterior	$^3\!/_4$"	4"	$21^1\!/_4$"	C	2
J exterior	$^3\!/_4$"	4"	$13^3\!/_8$"	C	2
K cleat	$^3\!/_4$"	$^3\!/_4$"	$19^3\!/_4$"	C	2
L cleat	$^3\!/_4$"	$^3\!/_4$"	$10^3\!/_8$"	C	2
M glue block	$^3\!/_4$"	$^3\!/_4$"	$3^1\!/_4$"	C	4
Two Doors					
N stile	$^3\!/_4$"	2"	$32^7\!/_8$"	C	4
O rail	$^3\!/_4$"	3"	16"	C	2
P rail	$^3\!/_4$"	2"	16"	C	2
Glass Stops					
Q* stop	$^1\!/_4$"	$^1\!/_4$"	$27^7\!/_8$"	C	8
R* stop	$^1\!/_4$"	$^1\!/_4$"	16"	C	8
S* stop	$^1\!/_4$"	$^1\!/_4$"	28"	C	16
T* stop	$^1\!/_4$"	$^1\!/_4$"	$8^3\!/_4$"	C	16

*Parts marked with an * are cut larger initially, then trimmed to finished size. Please read the instructions before cutting.

Material Key: C—cherry, CP—cherry plywood.

Supplies: #8x1$^1\!/_4$" flathead wood screws, #4x$^1\!/_2$" flathead wood screws, #18x$^1\!/_2$" brads, $^3\!/_8$" dowel pins $1^1\!/_2$" long, $^1\!/_4$" plate glass for the shelves, 4—$^1\!/_8$" glass for the side frames, stain, finish.

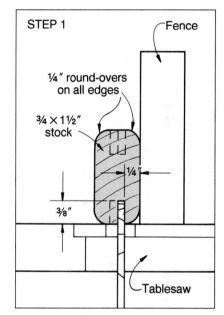

STEP 1

Fence

$^1\!/_4$" round-overs on all edges

$^3\!/_4$ × $1^1\!/_2$" stock

$^1\!/_4$"

$^3\!/_8$"

Tablesaw

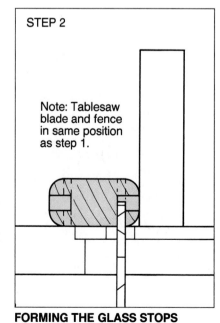

STEP 2

Note: Tablesaw blade and fence in same position as step 1.

FORMING THE GLASS STOPS

CHERRY CURIO CABINET
continued

quarter-round cherry stops from each 1½×36"-long strip. (We used a pushstick for safety when cutting the long, thin stops.)

3. Starting with one side panel, measure the opening and miter-cut the long glass stops (S).

4. Construct the jig shown *below.* Snip the head off a #18×½" brad and chuck it into your drill. Use the jig to position the stops in the front of the frame. Drill through the stop as shown in photo A *below.* Tap a brad into place in the hole just

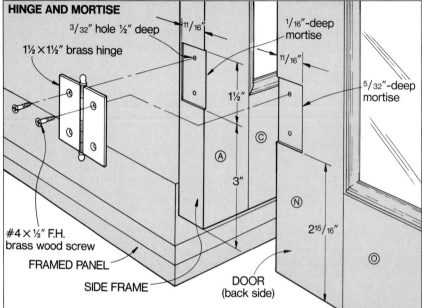

HINGE AND MORTISE

3/32" hole ½" deep

1½×1½" brass hinge

1/16"-deep mortise

11/16"

11/16"

5/32"-deep mortise

1½"

3"

2¹⁵/₁₆"

#4×½" F.H. brass wood screw

FRAMED PANEL

SIDE FRAME

DOOR (back side)

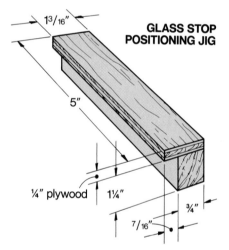

GLASS STOP POSITIONING JIG

1³/₁₆"

5"

¼" plywood   1¼"

¾"

7/16"

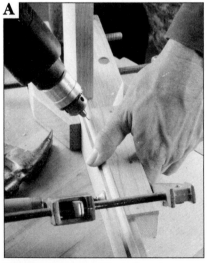

A

Use the jig to position the glass stops. Then drill pilot holes, and brad the stops into place.

drilled. Fasten the *outside* stops on each side frame and the *front* stops on both door frames; space the brads about 7" apart. Set the brads, and fill the holes with putty. (You'll need the remaining stops during final assembly, when you install the glass.)

Hang the doors

1. Mark the hinge locations on the front of the right-hand side frames as shown on the Hinge and Mortise Drawing, *above.*

2. Position the hinge on the marked outline. Mark the screw-hole locations. Drill pilot holes.

3. Screw the brass hinges to the side frames and score their outline into the frames as shown in photo B *right.* Then remove the hinges.

B

Screw the hinges to the cabinet. Next, scribe the hinge locations into the front of the side frame.

4. Chuck a ⅜" or ½" straight bit into your router. Clamp a piece of scrap stock to the inside edge of one of the side frames, making sure the top edges of the scrap stock and the frame are flush. The scrap stock helps support and level the router when routing the hinge mortise. Next, routing just *inside* the marked lines, rout ⅟₁₆"-deep mortises as shown in photo C *below.* Use a sharp chisel to finish cutting to the scribed hinge outline.

C

Clamp a piece of scrapwood to the front of the side frames for additional support, and rout the hinge mortises.

5. Clamp the doors into position in the cabinet front openings, and transfer the hinge locations onto the doors. Remove the doors from the cabinet, and finish marking the hinge outline. Using the routing and chiseling method just described, rout ⁵⁄₃₂"-deep mortises on the back side of each door frame.

Complete the assembly

1. Measure the openings and order glass cut to size for the four side panels, the two doors, and the three shelves. (We had the glass cut ⅟₁₆" less in length and width for the doors and side frames to allow for movement of the wood.)

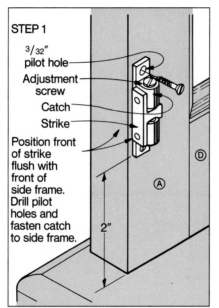

STEP 1

³/₃₂"
pilot hole

Adjustment screw

Catch

Strike

Position front of strike flush with front of side frame. Drill pilot holes and fasten catch to side frame.

2"

Ⓓ

Ⓐ

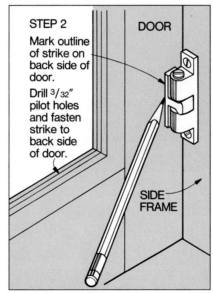

STEP 2

DOOR

Mark outline of strike on back side of door.

Drill ³/₃₂" pilot holes and fasten strike to back side of door.

SIDE FRAME

ATTACHING THE STRIKE AND CATCH

2. Locate and drill the holes for the doorknobs where shown on the Cabinet Assembly Drawing, page 32. Follow the Attaching the Strike and Catch Drawing *below* to attach the catches and strikes.

3. Position the glass, then carefully drill the holes and fasten the remaining cherry glass stops to the back side of each glass panel with brads. Set the nails and fill the holes.

4. Remove all the hardware from the cabinet and doors. Sand the wood parts smooth. Mask off both sides of the glass. Stain the cabinet and doors (we used cherry stain), and apply the finish of your choice.

5. Attach the two doors to the cabinet, place the cabinet against a wall, and add the glass shelves.

Buying Guide
• **Hardware.** 1½ × 1½" solid brass hinges, catalog no. 26476 (two pairs). Brass ball catches, catalog no. 28613 (two required). 1" brass knobs, catalog no. 35477 (two required). Brass shelf supports, catalog no. 30437 (12 required). To obtain current prices, contact The Woodworkers' Store, 21801 Industrial Blvd., Rogers, MN 55374-9514. Or call 612/428-2199.

TABLES, CHAIRS, AND DESKS

Choose from no fewer than three dining tables . . . build a complement of chairs to go with them . . . construct a handsome, raised-panel library desk. You could furnish several rooms in your home with the elegant projects that appear on the following pages.

EXPANDABLE OAK DINING TABLE AND CHAIRS

Have you been scouting for just the right table and chairs for your dining area? Look no further than the set *opposite*. Made to last, this refined, yet sturdy, dining ensemble will serve your family for years to come. First let's look at how the table goes together. Then turn to page 43 for step-by-step instructions for building the chairs.

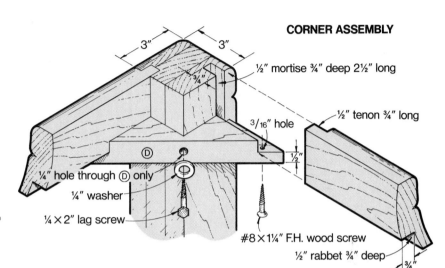

CORNER ASSEMBLY

½" mortise ¾" deep 2½" long

½" tenon ¾" long

3/16" hole

¾"

½"

¼" hole through Ⓓ only

¼" washer

¼ × 2" lag screw

#8 × 1¼" F.H. wood screw

½" rabbet ¾" deep

¾"

Table

Choose the natural beauty of an oak top, or opt for the added durability of laminate. Guests for dinner? No problem! Simply add a leaf . . . or two . . . or three to seat up to eight people comfortably.

Form the legs

1. To form the four legs, refer to the Cutting Diagram, page 39, then rip and crosscut 12 pieces (A) of 1⁄₁₆" stock 3¼" wide by 29" long. Glue and clamp three pieces together for each leg, keeping the ends and edges as flush as possible.

2. After the glue dries, scrape off the excess and plane one of the laminated edges smooth. Set this planed edge against the tablesaw fence and rip the leg to a 3" width. Now rip ¼" off either adjoining edge to form a 3 × 3" square leg. Crosscut each of the legs to 27½".

3. Lay out and mark the two mortises on one end of each leg as dimensioned on the Corner Assembly Drawing, *above right.*

4. Using a drill press with a ⅜" flat-bottomed bit, drill a series of ¾"-deep holes to remove most of the wood from the marked mortises as shown in photo A *above, center.* (We used a back

A

fence and stop, as shown, to ensure that all mortises were consistent in size and position. We also set the stop on the drill press to make sure that all holes were drilled to the same ¾" depth.) You will be able to drill one of the mortises in each leg with the setup shown. Move the stopblock to the other side of the bit, reclamp the stop to the fence, and drill the other leg mortises.

5. Using a fence on the router table and a stopblock clamped to the fence, rout the mortises clean with a ½" straight bit as shown in

B

photo B *above.* You'll be able to rout one mortise on each leg with the setup shown. Move and reclamp the stopblock to the other side of the bit, and proceed to rout the other mortises. Using a chisel and mallet, square the rounded ends of each mortise.

Build the base

1. Rip and crosscut the side aprons (B) and end aprons (C) to the sizes listed in the Bill of Materials, page 39.

2. Rabbet the ends of each apron to form ½" tenons ¾" long. (We cut ours on the radial-arm saw using a dado blade. We test-cut scrap material *continued*

EXPANDABLE OAK
DINING TABLE AND CHAIRS
continued

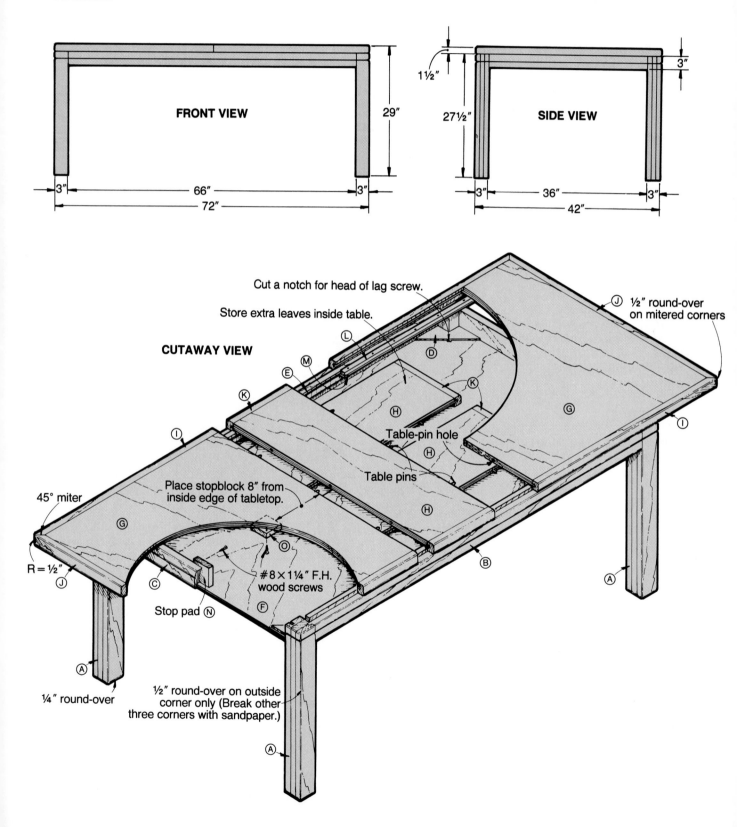

FRONT VIEW

29″

1½″

27½″

SIDE VIEW

3″

3″

3″

66″

72″

3″

3″

36″

42″

3″

Cut a notch for head of lag screw.

Store extra leaves inside table.

J ½″ round-over
on mitered corners

CUTAWAY VIEW

L

M

E

D

K

K

H

G

Table-pin hole

I

H

Table pins

H

45° miter

Place stopblock 8″ from
inside edge of tabletop.

G

B

A

R = ½″

J

C

O

#8 × 1¼″ F.H.
wood screws

Stop pad N

F

A

I

H

A

¼″ round-over

½″ round-over on outside
corner only (Break other
three corners with sandpaper.)

A

Bill of Materials

Part	Finished Size*			Mat.	Qty.
	T	W	L		
Table Base					
A* leg	1¹/₁₆″	3″	27½″	O	12
B side apron	1¹/₁₆″	3″	67½″	O	2
C end apron	1¹/₁₆″	3″	37½″	O	2
D* corner brace	1¹/₁₆″	5″	10″	O	4
E slide rail	1¹/₁₆″	1½″	66″	O	2
F panel	½″	41⅜″	71⅜″	PLY	1
Tabletop					
G panel	¾″	35⁷/₁₆″	40⅞″	OP	2
H leaf	¾″	12″	40⅞″	OP	3
I* edging	1¹/₁₆″	1½″	36″	O	4
J* edging	1¹/₁₆″	1½″	42″	O	2
K* edging	1¹/₁₆″	1½″	12″	O	6
L cleat	⅝″	¾″	34¹⁵/₁₆″	O	4
M runner	⅛″	1″	34¹⁵/₁₆″	FA	4
N stop pad	¾″	3″	3″	O	2
O stopblock	¾″	3″	3″	O	2

*Parts marked with an * are cut larger initially, then trimmed to finished size. Please read the instructions before cutting.

Material Key: O—oak, PLY—plywood, OP—oak plywood, FA—flat aluminum.
Supplies: #8x¾″ flathead wood screws, #8x1¼″ flathead wood screws, #8x1½″ flathead wood screws, 4—¼x2″ lag screws and washers, paraffin wax, ¹/₁₆″ laminate and contact cement (for laminate top only).

first and checked the fit of the tenon into the mortises.) The outside faces of the aprons should be flush with the outside faces of the legs when the tenon is installed in the mortise.

3. Cut a ½″ rabbet ¾″ deep along the bottom edge of each apron to the size and position indicated on the Corner Assembly Drawing, page 37, and the Section View Drawing, page 41.

4. Glue and clamp the side aprons (B) to the legs, checking for square. Remove any excess glue after it forms a tough skin. After both side assemblies (A, B) are dry, join them by gluing and clamping the end aprons (C) in position, again checking for square. *continued*

Cutting Diagram

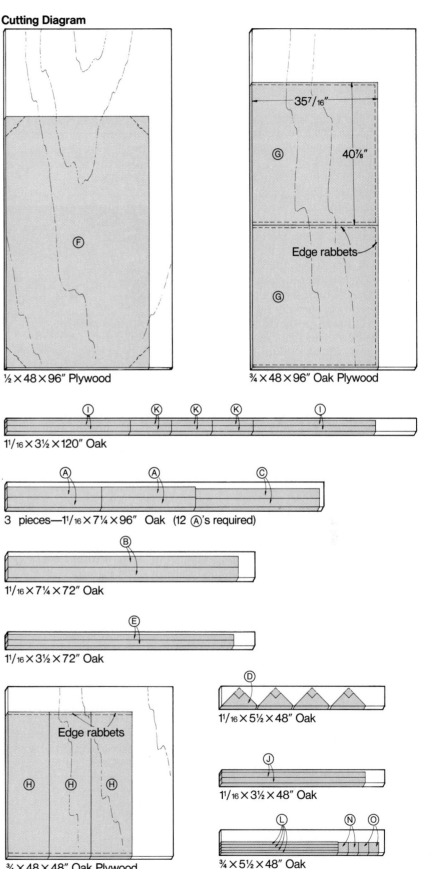

½ × 48 × 96″ Plywood

¾ × 48 × 96″ Oak Plywood

1¹/₁₆ × 3½ × 120″ Oak

3 pieces—1¹/₁₆ × 7¼ × 96″ Oak (12 Ⓐ's required)

1¹/₁₆ × 7¼ × 72″ Oak

1¹/₁₆ × 3½ × 72″ Oak

1¹/₁₆ × 5½ × 48″ Oak

1¹/₁₆ × 3½ × 48″ Oak

¾ × 5½ × 48″ Oak

¾ × 48 × 48″ Oak Plywood

EXPANDABLE OAK DINING TABLE AND CHAIRS
continued

***Note:** The table is rather fragile at this point. If you must move it, do so with care, and with the aid of a helper.*

5. Cut the corner braces (D) to size plus 1″ in length, noting the direction of the grain shown on the Corner Brace Drawing, *below,* to achieve maximum strength. *Do not* cut the notch yet. (We set our radial-arm-saw blade at 45° and made one cut on each of the four braces. We then reset the blade to 45° on the other side of center, set up a stopblock 10″ from the blade, and cut the braces to size.)

CORNER BRACE

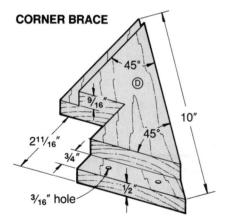

6. Using a dado blade, an auxiliary wood fence on the tablesaw, and a miter gauge, as shown in photo C *below,* cut a ¾″ rabbet ⁹⁄₁₆″ deep in one edge of each brace.

C

To cut the other rabbet in each brace, set the miter gauge at 45° right of center, and push the brace through the blade as shown in photo D *below.*

D

7. Notch the four braces (D) to fit around the inside corners of the legs. Drill four ³⁄₁₆″ holes in each brace for the #8 × 1¼″ screws. Hold each brace in position in the corner, and drill pilot holes into the bottom of the aprons. Glue and screw each brace into the rabbets in the apron as shown on the Corner Assembly Drawing, page 37. Now drill a ¼″ hole through each brace and just into the leg. Switch to a ³⁄₁₆″ bit and drill 1½″ into the corner of each leg. Install the ¼ × 2″ lag screws and washers through the braces and into the table legs.

8. Sand the leg-apron joints smooth, checking that the tops of the legs are flush with the top edge of each of the aprons.

9. Fit your router with a ½″ round-over bit and rout the top edges of the base and down the outside edge of each of the legs (round-over one edge only as shown on the Cutaway View Drawing, page 38).

10. Fit a router with a ⁹⁄₃₂″ point-cutting ogee bit and edge-guide fence as shown in photo E *below.* Locate the line of cut (1½″ from the top edge of the aprons as indicated on the Section View Drawing, *opposite, top*). Rout the decorative groove around the perimeter of the base.

E

11. Cut the slide rails (E) to size. Then cut a ⁵⁄₃₂″ groove ⁵⁄₁₆″ deep in both of the slide rails. The bottom of the groove should be ⁷⁄₁₆″ from the top edge of each slide. The bottom of the groove also should sit level with the top edge of the aprons when installed later, as shown on the Section View Drawing and on the Sliding Mechanism Drawing, *opposite, middle.*

12. Fasten the slide rails (E) to the side aprons with #8 × 1½″ wood screws. The bottom of the ⁵⁄₃₂″ groove in the slide rails must be ¼₆″ above the top edge of the legs, as shown on the Slide Rail Detail, *opposite, bottom left.* This ensures clearance when installing the aluminum runners in the grooved rails. Chamfer the top outside edge of the slide rails to prevent drag later.

13. Carefully turn the base upside down. Cut the plywood panel (F) to size. Cut the corners of the plywood to accommodate the corner braces (D). You'll

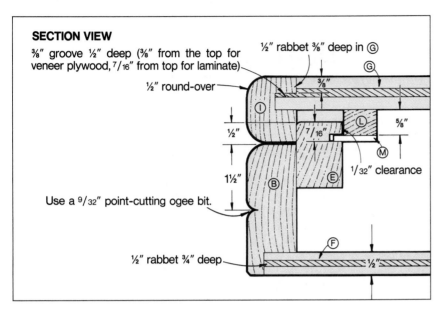

SECTION VIEW

⅜" groove ½" deep (⅜" from the top for veneer plywood, ⁷⁄₁₆" from top for laminate)

½" rabbet ⅜" deep in Ⓖ

Ⓖ

½" round-over

Ⓘ

⅜"

Ⓛ

⁵⁄₈"

½"

⁷⁄₁₆"

Ⓜ

¹⁄₃₂" clearance

1½"

Ⓑ

Ⓔ

Use a ⁹⁄₃₂" point-cutting ogee bit.

½" rabbet ¾" deep

Ⓕ

½"

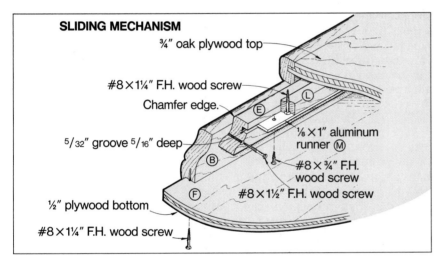

SLIDING MECHANISM

¾" oak plywood top

#8×1¼" F.H. wood screw

Chamfer edge.

Ⓛ

Ⓔ

⁵⁄₃₂" groove ⁵⁄₁₆" deep

⅛×1" aluminum runner Ⓜ

Ⓑ

#8×¾" F.H. wood screw

½" plywood bottom

Ⓕ

#8×1½" F.H. wood screw

#8×1¼" F.H. wood screw

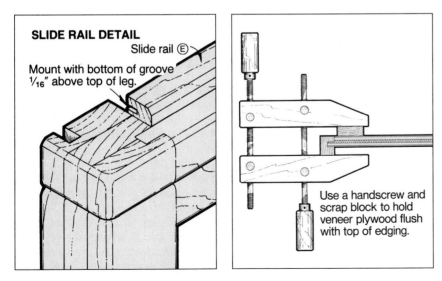

SLIDE RAIL DETAIL

Slide rail Ⓔ

Mount with bottom of groove ¹⁄₁₆" above top of leg.

Use a handscrew and scrap block to hold veneer plywood flush with top of edging.

need to cut a small notch in each mitered corner for the head of the corner-brace lag screw. Drill pilot holes and fasten (but *do not* glue) the plywood panel to the base to test the fit. Remove the plywood panel; it will be reinstalled later.

14. With the base upside down, use a ¼" round-over bit to rout the bottom edges of each leg. Sand the entire base assembly.

Build the top and leaves

1. Cut the plywood top panels (G) and leaves (H) to size, as indicated in the Bill of Materials, page 39, and as laid out on the Cutting Diagram, page 39. It is important to note the direction of the grain *before* cutting: The grain runs across the table, not the length of it.

2. Cut a ½" rabbet ⅜" deep along three edges of each top panel (G) and along both ends of each leaf (H) to form a tongue, as shown on the Section View Drawing, *top left,* and on the Cutting Diagram. (To reduce chip-out, we made the cross-grain cuts first, then those with the grain. We also used a feather board clamped to the fence to keep the oak veneer running flat across the blade.)

3. Rip the oak edging I, J, and K to 1½", then crosscut the pieces to length plus 2".

4. Cut a ⅜" groove ½" deep along all edging pieces (I, J, K) to accept the tongue on the plywood. Test-cut scrap material first to ensure that the edging fits over the tongue, snugly against the veneer, and, most important, flush with the veneer surface of the plywood top.

5. Miter-cut both ends of each J to length. Then miter-cut the mating end of each I piece and crosscut the other ends to length.

6. Glue and clamp the edging to the panels and leaves, checking that the miters pull tight. If the tabletop appears to be higher than the edging in spots, clamp a piece of scrap to the panel and edging, as shown on the drawing, *near left.* *continued*

EXPANDABLE OAK DINING TABLE AND CHAIRS
continued

7. After the glue dries, *carefully* remove the excess, and sand or scrape the edging flush with the veneer top. (We used a cabinet scraper and were *extremely* careful not to scrape through the thin veneer.)

8. Using a ½″ round-over bit, rout the outside top, bottom, and corner edges (where the miters meet) of the top sections. *Do not* rout the edges that meet when the table sections close.

Make the tabletop slide smoothly

1. Position the two tabletop panels (G) facedown on a blanket spread on a flat surface (to prevent scratching). Align the halves so that they butt uniformly. Position the base (also upside down) on the panels, and place ¹⁄₁₆″ spacers between the aprons (B, C) and the edging (I, J) as shown on the drawing, *below.* This ensures that the edging sits ¹⁄₁₆″ above the top of the aprons and legs, and helps avoid the friction that could occur when the tabletop slides.

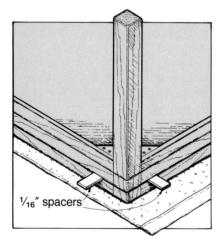

¹⁄₁₆″ spacers

2. Cut the aluminum runners (M) to length. Sand or file the corners at a slight radius to remove burrs caused by cutting and to further ensure a smooth

slide. Drill and countersink holes through the runners for #8 × ¾″ screws to attach the runners (M) to the cleats (L).

3. Insert the aluminum runners into the ⁵⁄₃₂″ groove in E, and measure the distance between the bottom of the tabletop and the top of the runners for the correct thickness of the spacer. Ours measured ⅝″ (see the Section View Drawing, page 41, for help with this). Cut the cleats to size.

4. Align the cleats (L) alongside the slide rails (E) and secure them to the bottom of the tabletop with #8 × 1¼″ screws. Now fasten the runners (M) to the spacers. Take your time aligning and fastening these parts; the outcome will determine how easily your tabletop slides.

5. Center and fasten the stop pads (N) to the inside edge of each end apron. Measure in 8″ from the inside or closing edge of each half of the tabletop and fasten the stopblocks (O) to the bottom of the tabletop halves.

6. With the aid of a helper, turn the table right side up. Lay out and mark the position of three table pins in one of the tabletop halves. Using a doweling jig to ensure that the holes are drilled straight, drill ⅜″ holes ¹¹⁄₁₆″ deep. Insert dowel centers and bring the halves together with the edges aligned.

Drill corresponding holes in the other tabletop half, and insert (but don't glue) the pins to check for a proper fit with the halves closed. If the pins align properly, remove them and use this same procedure to mark and drill the leaves. Once all the holes are drilled, glue the pins in place.

7. Remove the stop pads (N) from the bottom of the tabletop. Slide the tabletop sections off the base. (The table is easier to finish with the top off.)

Finish and assemble

1. Finish-sand the entire base assembly, and break any sharp edges on the legs and on the bottom of the aprons. Finish-sand the tabletop halves and leaves.

2. Mask the aluminum runners to prevent getting any finish on them. Stain, if desired, and finish the base, tabletop halves, and leaves. Be sure to finish both the bottom and top of the tabletop halves and leaves. (We left the oak natural and finished it with several coats of polyurethane.)

3. Wipe a bit of paraffin wax onto the aluminum runners (M) and into the groove in the rail. The paraffin wax will lubricate the moving parts, helping to reduce friction and ensure smooth-sliding parts.

4. Reattach the top to the base and reinstall the stop pads (N). Again with the aid of a helper, turn the table upside down, being careful not to scratch the finish. Refasten the plywood panel (F) to the bottom of the table and stand the table back on its feet.

Buying Guide

• **Table pins.** ⅜″-diameter by 1¼″-long wood pins, catalog no. 21253. To obtain the current price, contact The Woodworkers' Store, 21801 Industrial Blvd., Rogers, MN 55374-9514. Or call 612/428-2199.

• **⁹⁄₃₂″ point-cutting ogee bit.** Stock no. 9GT26323. Available at Sears stores.

• **Aluminum stock.** ⅛ × 1 × 96″ rectangular stock. Macklanburg-Duncan stock no. 0741-3123. You can purchase M-D parts at or through Ace Hardware Stores, Payless Cashways Home Centers, and other stores.

Chair

No woodworking project demands more attention to snug joinery and properly scaled dimensions than a chair. We've taken special pains to ensure that this sturdy oak dining chair will remain comfortable and eye-pleasing for years to come.

Note: The instructions explain how to make one chair, and the Bill of Materials, page 44, gives the number of pieces required for one chair. You will need to determine how many chairs you want, then cut and machine as many parts as necessary. When making four or six chairs, cut all identical pieces at the same time. We tried upholstering our own chairs with mixed results; you may be better off having a professional do the upholstering for you.

Form the legs

1. Referring to the Cutting Diagram, page 44, cut the front legs (A) to size. (You can use 1½" stock or laminate two ¾" pieces together.)

2. To make the back legs (B), start by cutting two 1¹/₁₆"-thick pieces 4⅛" wide by 36" long. Using the Back/Leg Drawing, *below left,* lay out and mark the shape of just *one* of the back legs. With the aid of a helper, use a flexible thin strip of wood to mark the curved lines.

3. Lay out and mark the position of the mortises on the front and back legs as dimensioned on the Leg-Rail Assembly Drawing, *below right,* and on the Back/Leg Drawing.

Note: Remember that you are working in pairs (pairs of front legs and pairs of back legs). You'll want to mark the mortises on each pair before cutting to ensure that you machine the
correct side of each part. (We marked one right leg and one left leg and used these as templates to mark the rest of the legs.) We also taped the pairs together after each marking and machining.

4. To form the mortises in the front legs, use a drill press with a ⅜" flat-bottomed bit, and drill out the stock within the marked mortise lines ½" deep, as shown in photo A, page 45. You can drill one of the mortises in each front leg with the setup shown. You then must move and reclamp the stopblock to the other side of the bit, and drill the other mortises in each leg. Marking the mortise locations earlier prevents confusion here. We used a back fence and stop to ensure that all the mortises were consistent in size and location. And we set the stop on the drill press to make sure that all holes were drilled to the same depth.

continued

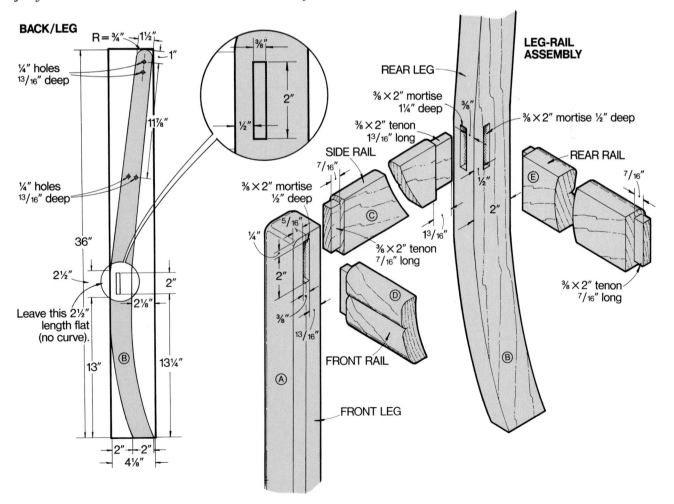

EXPANDABLE OAK
DINING TABLE AND CHAIRS
continued

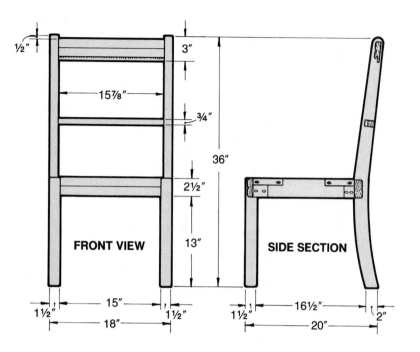

½"

3"

15⅞"

¾"

36"

2½"

13"

FRONT VIEW

15"

1½"   1½"

18"

SIDE SECTION

1½"   16½"   2"

20"

EXPLODED VIEW

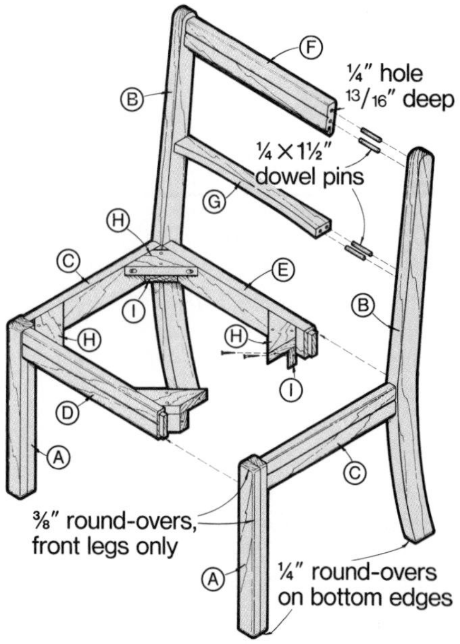

¼" hole
¹³/₁₆" deep

¼ × 1½"
dowel pins

⅜" round-overs,
front legs only

¼" round-overs
on bottom edges

Cutting Diagram (For one chair)

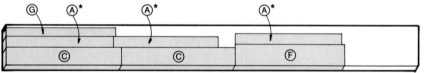

¾ × 5½ × 60" Oak   *Note: We laminated 2 Ⓐ's to form each front leg.

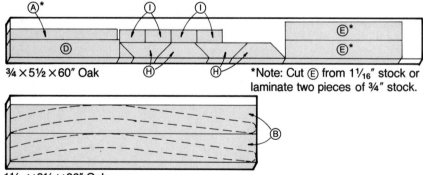

¾ × 5½ × 60" Oak   *Note: Cut Ⓔ from 1¹/₁₆" stock or
laminate two pieces of ¾" stock.

1¹/₁₆ × 9¼ × 36" Oak

Bill of Materials

Part	Finished Size			Mat.	Qty.
	T	W	L		
A front leg	1½"	1½"	15½"	O	2
B back leg	1¹/₁₆"	4⅛"	36"	O	2
C side rail	¾"	2½"	16⅛"	O	2
D front rail	¾"	2½"	15⅞"	O	1
E back rail	1¹/₁₆"	2½"	16¾"	O	1
F upper backrest	¾"	3"	15⅞"	O	1
G backrest rail	¾"	1¼"	15⅞"	O	1
H corner brace	¾"	2⅛"	7½"	O	4
I corner brace	¾"	1¾"	3¾"	O	4
J seat	½"	16"	17"	PLY	1
K backrest panel	¼"	15¾"	10¾"	HB	1
L staple cleat	½"	½"	9¾"	P	2

Material Key: O—oak, PLY—plywood,
HB—hardboard, P—pine.
Supplies: #8x1" flathead wood screws,
#8x1½" flathead wood screws, ¼x1½" dowel
pins, ½" foam padding, fabric, Stanley 1"
corner braces (no. CD997), staples.

A

5. Drill the mortises in the front of the back legs the same way the front ones were drilled. However, note that you will need to construct a longer fence with stops for your drill-press table.

6. Using a double fence (shown in photo B, *below*) on the router table to ensure a perfectly straight routed groove, and a ⅜" straight bit, rout the mortises clean in each leg. Use a stop to ensure a consistent mortise length. You'll be able to rout one mortise on each leg front with the setup shown. Move and reclamp the stopblock to the other side of the bit, and rout the other drilled mortises clean.

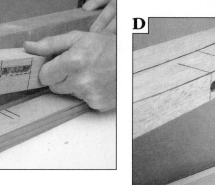

B

7. Use the same double fence on the router table and the same ⅜" bit ½" above the surface of the table. Adjust the fences and stops and rout the mortises clean (1¼" deep) in the front edge of each back leg, as shown in photo C, *below*. Make at least two passes to achieve the 1¼" depth and not strain the bit.

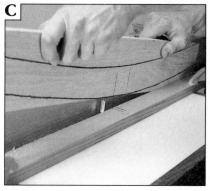

C

(As shown in photo C, we marked the length of the mortise on the side of each rear leg, and marked the location of the router bit on the front fence. The marks on the fence indicate the exact position of the ⅜" bit. This enabled us to rout the mortise to exact size, despite the fact that this is a "blind-routing" operation. Using the marks, you can eliminate the use of a long back fence and stops.) Photo D, *below,* shows the routed mortise.

8. Drill the mortise in the inside face of each leg. Then,

D

back at the router table, adjust the fence, stops, and depth of cut, and rout the mortises clean.

9. Use a sharp chisel and a mallet to square the rounded ends of each routed mortise.

10. With a bandsaw, cut the previously marked back leg to shape, cutting just slightly outside the line drawn. Now sand the leg to the marked line. Using this leg as a template, mark the shape of the other back leg. Then cut and sand it to shape. (Accurately shaping the first leg ensures a good template for tracing the other legs.)

Machine the rails

1. Rip and crosscut the side rails (C), front rail (D), and back rail (E) to size as listed in the Bill of Materials, *opposite*. Note that the back rail is longer than the front, as shown on the drawing, *below.*

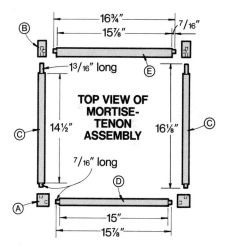

16¾"	7/16"
15⅞"	

13/16" long — ⒺＥ

ⒷＢ

14½" — ©C

TOP VIEW OF MORTISE-TENON ASSEMBLY

16⅛" — ©C

7/16" long

ⒹＤ

ⒶＡ

15"
15⅞"

2. Cut the ends of each rail to form tenons as dimensioned on the Leg-Rail Assembly Drawing, page 43. (We did ours on the radial-arm saw using a dado blade. We cut our tenons 1/16" less than the depth of the mortise to allow for glue pocketing. We test-cut scrap material first, and checked the fit of the test tenon into the mortises previously machined in the legs.) *continued*

EXPANDABLE OAK DINING TABLE AND CHAIRS
continued

3. Cut the backrest rails (F, G) to size. (Use the Lower Backrest Drawing, *top right,* as a guide to mark and cut the shallow recess on the front edge of G.)

4. Using the Rails and Upper Backrest Drawing, *near right, center,* lay out and mark the location of the ⁹⁄₃₂″ ogee cuts on the rails (C, D, E) and upper backrest (F). Also lay out the ¼″ groove you'll be cutting in the bottom of the upper backrest (F). Fit your table-mounted router with a ⁹⁄₃₂″ point-cutting ogee bit, and set up a fence to guide the cut as shown in photo E *below.* Rout the decorative groove in the rails (C, D, E) and the upper backrest (F).

E

5. To cut the groove in the bottom edge of F, start by fitting your tablesaw with a dado blade. Move the fence ¼″ from the inside edge of the blade. The first cut should be ¼″ wide by ¾″ deep along the bottom edge of F. For the second cut, switch back to a ⅛″ blade set ⅜″ above the surface of the table with the outside edge of the blade ½″ from the fence.

6. To round over the top and bottom edges of the upper backrest (F), use the point-cutting ogee and a fence on your router table. Using a ⅜″ round-over bit, round over the edges of the front, side, and rear rails (C,

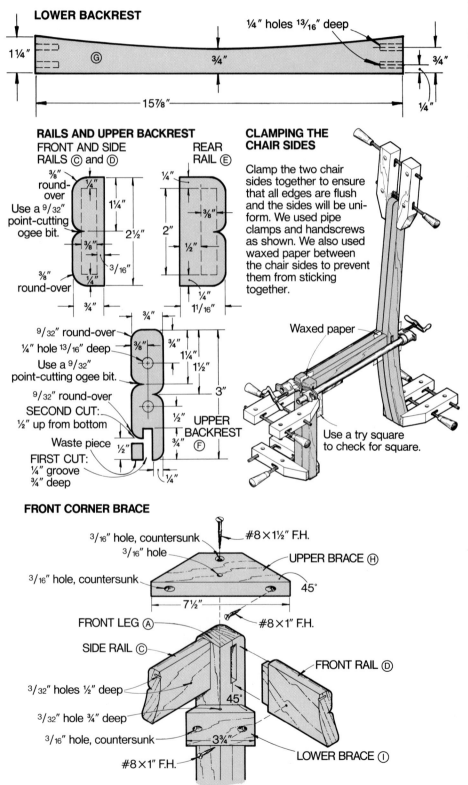

LOWER BACKREST

¼″ holes ¹³⁄₁₆″ deep

1¼″   Ⓖ   ¾″   ¾″

15⅞″   ¼″

RAILS AND UPPER BACKREST

FRONT AND SIDE RAILS Ⓒ and Ⓓ

⅜″ round-over
Use a ⁹⁄₃₂″ point-cutting ogee bit.
¼″
1¼″
⅜″
2½″
⅜″
³⁄₁₆″
⅜″ round-over
¼″
¾″

REAR RAIL Ⓔ

¼″
⅜″
2″
½″
¼″
1¹⁄₁₆″

¾″

⁹⁄₃₂″ round-over
¼″ hole ¹³⁄₁₆″ deep
Use a ⁹⁄₃₂″ point-cutting ogee bit.
⁹⁄₃₂″ round-over
SECOND CUT: ½″ up from bottom
Waste piece
FIRST CUT: ¼″ groove ¾″ deep

⅜″
¾″
1¼″
1½″
3″
½″
¾″
¼″
½″
UPPER BACKREST Ⓕ

CLAMPING THE CHAIR SIDES

Clamp the two chair sides together to ensure that all edges are flush and the sides will be uniform. We used pipe clamps and handscrews as shown. We also used waxed paper between the chair sides to prevent them from sticking together.

Waxed paper

Use a try square to check for square.

FRONT CORNER BRACE

³⁄₁₆″ hole, countersunk
³⁄₁₆″ hole
³⁄₁₆″ hole, countersunk
#8×1½″ F.H.
UPPER BRACE Ⓗ
45°
7½″
#8×1″ F.H.
FRONT LEG Ⓐ
SIDE RAIL Ⓒ
FRONT RAIL Ⓓ
³⁄₃₂″ holes ½″ deep
45°
³⁄₃₂″ hole ¾″ deep
³⁄₁₆″ hole, countersunk
3¾″
LOWER BRACE Ⓘ
#8×1″ F.H.

D, E), as indicated on the Rails and Upper Backrest Drawing.

7. Using the same ⅜" round-over bit, rout the front outside and top outside edges of the front legs, as indicated on the Exploded View Drawing, page 44. Rout a ¼" round-over on the bottom of all legs.

8. Using a doweling jig, drill ¼" holes 1³⁄₁₆" deep in the ends of the backrest rails (F, G), as indicated on the Rails and Upper Backrest and Lower Backrest drawings.

Assemble the chair

1. Glue and clamp the two mating chair sides together, as shown on the Clamping the Chair Sides Drawing, *opposite, center right,* checking for square.

2. After the glue dries, remove the clamps and excess glue. Chisel the remaining mortises in the back legs to their original ½" depth. The mortises have been partially filled in by the tenon of the side rails (C).

3. Dry-clamp the front and back rails (D, E) to join the two chair sides together. Check the fit of pieces F and G between the back legs. (Part G should be positioned flush with the back edge of B.)

4. Loosen the clamps slightly. Using ¼" dowel centers (you'll need to buy two sets of dowel centers for this project) in the ends of F, correctly position F between the back legs. Once positioned, compress the back legs together to transfer the dowel center's mark into the back legs. Repeat this process for the backrest rail (G).

5. Remove the clamps, and drill ¼" holes ¹³⁄₁₆" deep at the marks on the back legs. A doweling jig helps ensure that you locate the hole correctly.

6. Glue and insert the dowels, then glue and clamp the two chair sides together with the front and back rails (D, E), and backrest rails (F, G). Check that the rails are square with the legs and make sure that the chair is sitting on a perfectly flat surface while clamping.

7. Referring to the Front Corner Brace Drawing, *opposite, bottom,* cut the corner braces (H and I) to size. (We found that a couple of corner braces didn't fit, as the chair was a bit out of square. To correct this, we cut the braces slightly larger, scribed the angles needed, then recut the pieces for an exact fit.)

8. Clamp the corner braces in position as shown on the Exploded View Drawing, page 44. Then drill the pilot holes, and glue and screw the upper braces (H) in place. Follow the same procedure to mount the lower braces (I). Fasten H to I with a #8×1½" wood screw.

Make the cushions

1. Cut the plywood seat (J) to size. Radius the front corners, and notch the back corners, as shown in the Seat Cushion Drawing *below, top.* Bore 1" vent holes through the plywood. Sand or rout a slight round-over on the plywood's top and bottom edges.

2. Cut two pieces of ½"-thick foam padding to the same size as the plywood seat. Cover the seat (J) and foam with fabric.

SEAT CUSHION

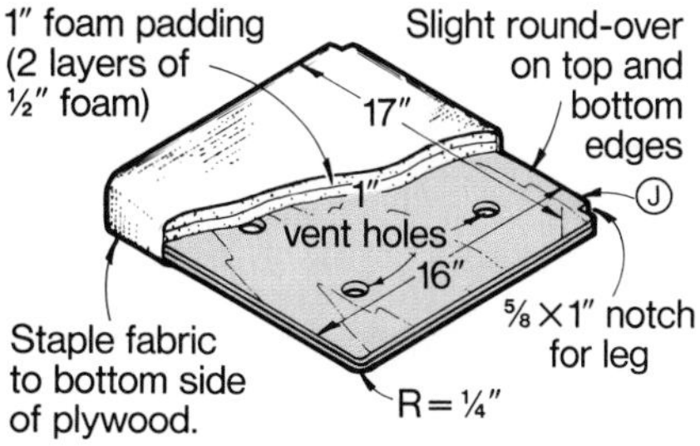
1" foam padding
(2 layers of
½" foam)
Slight round-over
on top and
bottom
edges
17"
1"
vent holes
16"
J
⅝×1" notch
for leg
Staple fabric
to bottom side
of plywood.
R=¼"

SEAT BACK

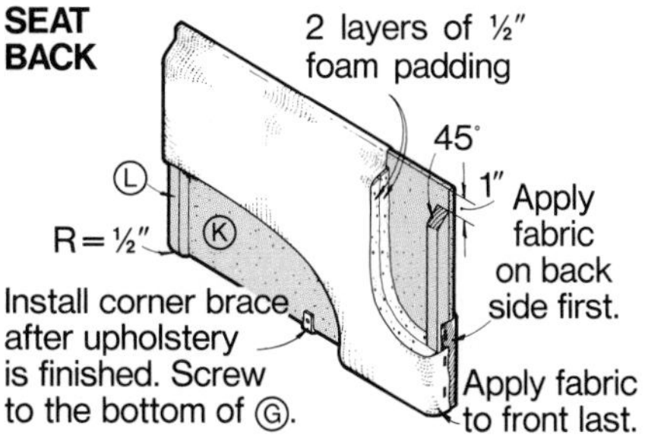
2 layers of ½"
foam padding
45°
1"
Apply
fabric
on back
side first.
L
R=½"
K
Install corner brace
after upholstery
is finished. Screw
to the bottom of G.
Apply fabric
to front last.

3. Cut the backrest panel (K) and pine staple cleats (L) to size. Bevel the top end and radius the bottom end of each cleat as shown on the Seat Back Drawing, *below left, bottom.*

4. Glue and clamp the pine cleats to the hardboard panel flush with the bottom and outside edges.

5. Cut two pieces of ½"-thick foam padding—the first to fit between the cleats and the second to overlap the cleats. Attach the fabric to the panel and cleat assembly as shown on the Seat Back Drawing.

Finish the chair and complete the assembly

1. Sand the entire chair assembly smooth, breaking any sharp edges with sandpaper. Finish the chair as desired. (We used polyurethane.)

2. After the finish is completely dry, turn the chair upside down on a clean work surface. Drill pilot holes and fasten the seat-cushion assembly to the corner braces with screws.

3. To achieve the curve in the lower part of the backrest, make a small cut (½" long) in the fabric along the bottom edge of the upholstered back, just in front of the hardboard. Then slip the top part of the upholstered back into the groove in the upper backrest. Press the hardboard back against the lower curved backrest (G) and clamp in position.

Insert a metal corner brace in the cut and in front of the hardboard as shown on the Seat Back Drawing. Then screw the brace to the bottom side of G to secure the hardboard firmly against the backrest. (We used the metal braces in the chairs we upholstered; an upholsterer used brads to fasten and bend the hardboard to the curved lower backrest, eliminating the need for a metal brace.)

Buying Guide

- **⁹⁄₃₂" point-cutting ogee bit.** Stock no. 9GT26323. Available at Sears stores.

SUNBURST DINING TABLE

Sit back and enjoy feasts and festivities on this matched-grain oak table supported by an attractive walnut-striped base. It makes a handsome centerpiece in any dining room. And, despite its impressive looks, the 48″ table is surprisingly easy to make. Simply lay out the pattern on plywood, then cut the parts with your router.

Begin with the base

Note: You'll need some ⅛″ walnut for this project. You can either resaw or plane thicker stock to the correct thickness.

Cut and laminate the legs

1. Cut the leg parts (A, B, C) to size plus ½″ in width and 1″ in length from ¾″ oak and ⅛″ walnut stock.

2. Spread an even coat of glue on the mating surfaces, then clamp eight A–B laminations together as shown on the drawing at *right*. Now glue and

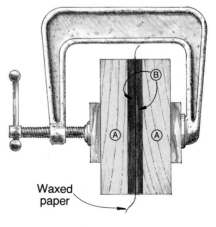

Waxed paper

clamp four C–C laminations together for the legs. (We used a 2″ disposable paint roller to apply the glue.)

3. Plane the *oak* face of each A–B lamination to reduce the total thickness to ¾″. (As shown on the drawing *below,* we used a pushblock and pushstick, and made several shallow cuts on the jointer to safely plane the lamination to size.)

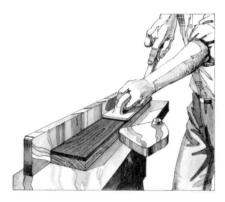

4. Trim the C–C laminations to a finished length of 21″. Glue and clamp a C–C lamination centered from end to end between a pair of A–Bs for each of the four legs; make sure the edges are flush.

5. After the glue dries, remove the clamps and scrape off the excess glue from *one* edge of each lamination. Set the tablesaw fence 3⅜″ from the blade, and with the scraped edge against the fence, rip *one* edge of each of the four legs. Now position the tablesaw fence 3¼″ from the blade and rip the *opposite edge* to cut the legs to finished width.

6. Finally, crosscut the legs to length so the open mortise on each end of each leg measures 3¼″ long. Remove any excess glue from the mortises with a sharp chisel.

Cut and laminate the feet

1. To cut and laminate the feet (D, E, F), use the same procedure outlined in steps 1, 2, and 3 of the previous section.

2. Trim one end of the four F–F laminations square. Glue and clamp each of them between a

pair of D–E laminations, with the D–E laminations flush with each other and 3¼″ from the squared end of the Fs as shown *below.*

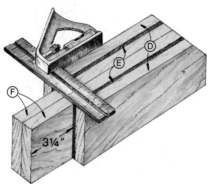

3¼″

3. Again, using the two-step ripping procedure used on the legs (see step 5 of the previous section), rip the feet to width (3¼″). Crosscut the feet to length (12″). Remove any excess glue from the tenons.

4. Cut the large chamfer on the end of each leg (we cut ours on the radial-arm saw).

Form the cross members and tabletop support

1. Cut the outside cross-member parts (G) to size plus ½″ in width, and cut the inside parts (H) to size plus ½″ in width and 1″ in length.

2. Glue and clamp the two H–H laminations together. Later, trim both ends of both laminations for a finished length of 18½″.

3. Glue and clamp an H–H lamination between two Gs for each cross member. Keep the ends of the two outer pieces flush with each other, using the same squaring technique used with the feet (as explained in step 2 of the previous section).

4. Cut a 3″-wide notch 1⅝″ deep centered along the length of each cross member where shown on the Exploded View Drawing, page 51.

5. Cut the support pieces (I, J) to size. Cut or rout a 45° chamfer on both ends of I and on one end of each J. Put the support pieces aside for now; you'll use them later on.

Assemble the base

1. Glue and clamp one foot to each leg, checking for square.

2. Glue and clamp two legs to one of the cross members, making sure the cross-member notch faces *up,* again checking for square. Repeat with the other two legs and cross member, making sure the cross-member notch faces *down.*

3. Interlock the two notched cross members, and glue and clamp the two leg assemblies together to form the base.

4. Center and clamp the tabletop support pieces to the top of the oak base. To mount the supports to the base, drill screw holes from the top side of the support pieces to the sizes noted on the Exploded View Drawing. Then screw the supports to the base assembly with wood screws.

Build the top

Note: To rout the plywood top and oak band, you'll need sharp carbide-tipped bits. Make several passes, lowering the bit no more than ¼″ per pass, to make each of the cuts.

Form the plywood top

1. Start by cutting a sheet of 4×8′ oak veneer plywood in half where shown on Step 1 of the Cutting Diagram, page 50.

2. Draw a diagonal line on both 4×4′ pieces of the oak plywood. (We laid the plywood on a half sheet of particleboard because the last routing cut needs to go into the particleboard about ⅛″ for a clean cut through the plywood. We used a router instead of a saw because routing causes less chipping.) Now clamp a straight board to the plywood, fit your router with a ½″ carbide-tipped straight bit, and rout down the center of the marked diagonal to cut both half sheets in half again (see Step 2 of the Cutting Diagram). *continued*

SUNBURST DINING TABLE
continued

Cutting Diagram

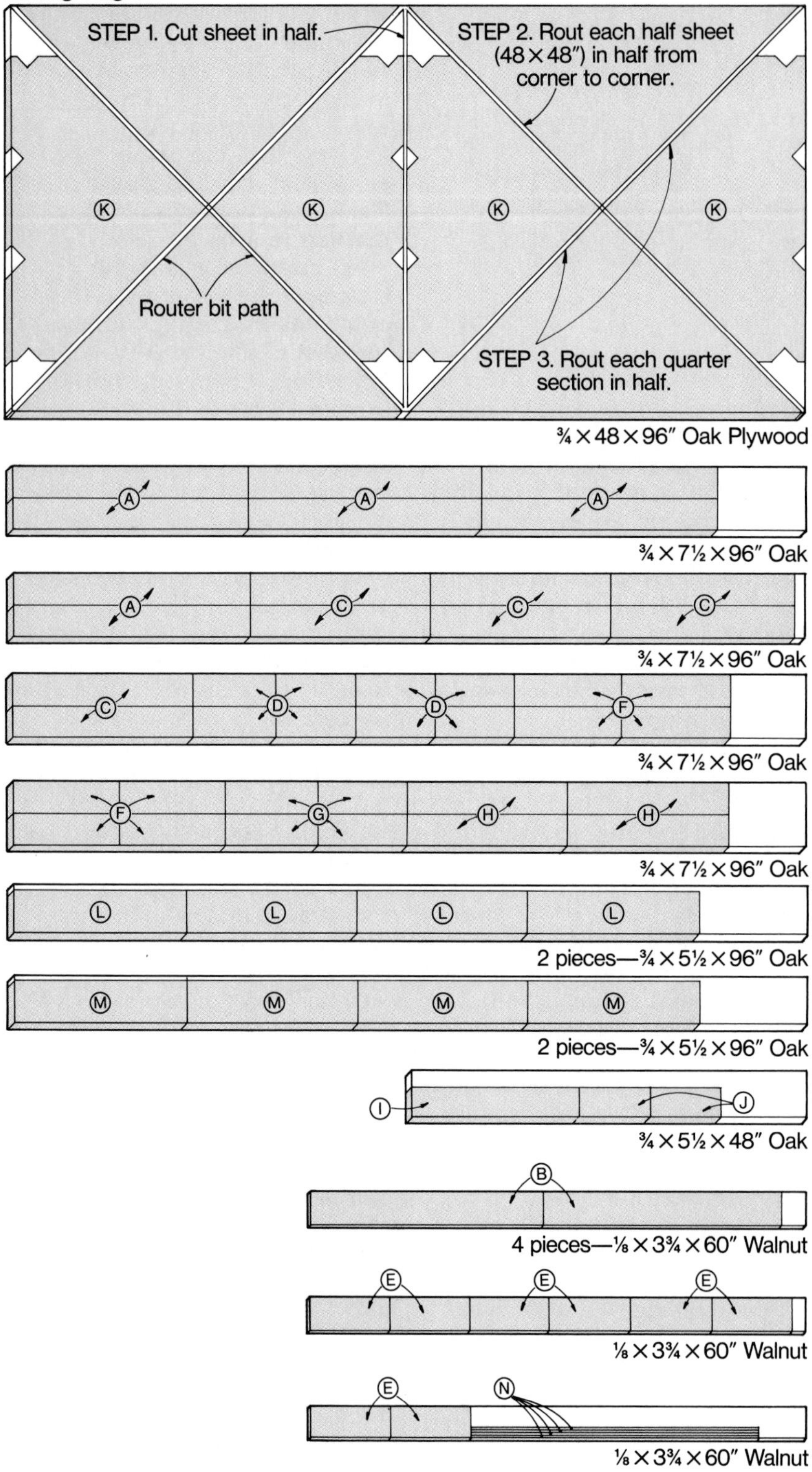
STEP 1. Cut sheet in half.
STEP 2. Rout each half sheet (48 × 48″) in half from corner to corner.
K
K
K
K
Router bit path
STEP 3. Rout each quarter section in half.
¾ × 48 × 96″ Oak Plywood
A
A
A
¾ × 7½ × 96″ Oak
A
C
C
C
¾ × 7½ × 96″ Oak
C
D
D
F
¾ × 7½ × 96″ Oak
F
G
H
H
¾ × 7½ × 96″ Oak
L
L
L
L
2 pieces—¾ × 5½ × 96″ Oak
M
M
M
M
2 pieces—¾ × 5½ × 96″ Oak
I
J
¾ × 5½ × 48″ Oak
B
4 pieces—⅛ × 3¾ × 60″ Walnut
E
E
E
⅛ × 3¾ × 60″ Walnut
E
N
⅛ × 3¾ × 60″ Walnut

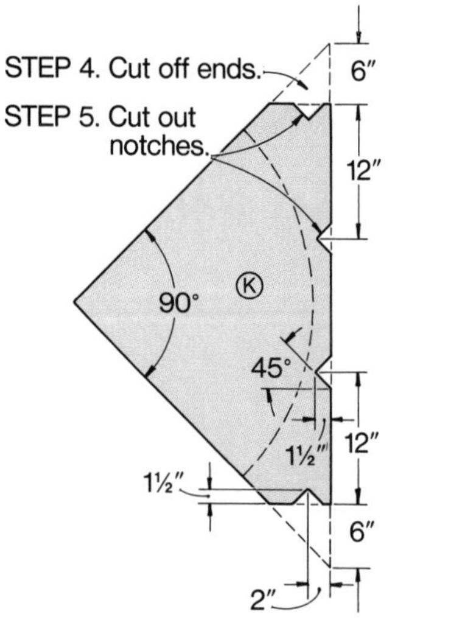
STEP 4. Cut off ends.
STEP 5. Cut out notches.
6″
12″
90°
K
45°
1½″
12″
1½″
6″
2″

PLYWOOD SECTION (TOP VIEW)

Bill of Materials

Part	Finished Size*			Mat.	Qty.
	T	W	L		
A* leg	¾″	3¼″	27½″	O	8
B* leg	⅛″	3¼″	27½″	W	8
C* leg	¾″	3¼″	21″	O	8
D* foot	¾″	3¼″	8¾″	O	8
E* foot	⅛″	3¼″	8¾″	W	8
F* foot	¾″	3¼″	12″	O	8
G* outside cross	¾″	3¼″	12″	O	4
H* inside cross	¾″	3¼″	18½″	O	4
I support	¾″	3½″	20½″	O	1
J support	¾″	3½″	8½″	O	2
K* top	¾″	36″	24″	OP	4
L* upper band	¾″	5¼″	20⅜″	O	8
M* lower band	¾″	5¼″	20⅜″	O	8
N* strip	⅛″	¾″	34⁹⁄₁₆″	W	4

*Parts marked with an * are cut larger initially, then trimmed to finished size. Please read the instructions before cutting.

Material Key: O—oak, W—walnut, OP—oak plywood.

Supplies: # 10 × 1¼″ flathead wood screws, ½″ dowel stock, 4—floor glides, stain (if desired), finish.

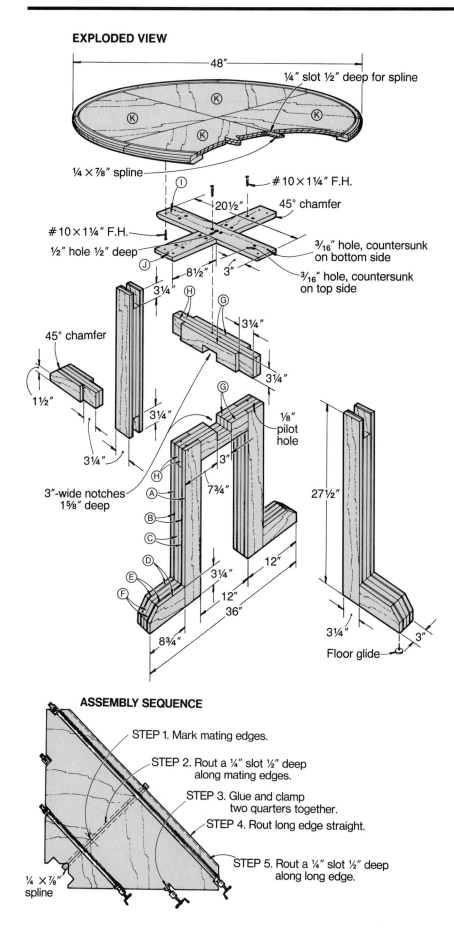

EXPLODED VIEW

48"

¼" slot ½" deep for spline

K K K K

¼ × ⅞" spline

#10 × 1¼" F.H.

20½"

45° chamfer

#10 × 1¼" F.H.

I

½" hole ½" deep

J

8½"   3"

3/16" hole, countersunk on bottom side

3/16" hole, countersunk on top side

3¼"

H

G

3¼"

45° chamfer

3¼"

G

H

3¼"

1½"

⅛" pilot hole

3¼"

3"

H

A

7¾"

B

C

D

E

F

3¼"

3"-wide notches 1⅝" deep

12"

27½"

12"

36"

8¾"

3¼"

3¼"   3"

Floor glide

ASSEMBLY SEQUENCE

STEP 1. Mark mating edges.

STEP 2. Rout a ¼" slot ½" deep along mating edges.

STEP 3. Glue and clamp two quarters together.

STEP 4. Rout long edge straight.

STEP 5. Rout a ¼" slot ½" deep along long edge.

¼ × ⅞" spline

3. Reposition your fence and rout the four triangular pieces in half where shown on Step 3 of the Cutting Diagram.

4. Referring to the Plywood Section Drawing, *opposite, top right,* use a jigsaw to cut off the ends of each plywood section (K) where shown on Step 4. Cut the notches where shown on Step 5 of the drawing.

Join the plywood pieces

1. Arrange the four plywood sections (K) to achieve the best grain pattern, and mark the mating edges where shown on Step 1 of the Assembly Sequence Drawing *below left.* Now rout a ¼" slot ½" deep along the mating edges of the two adjacent panels where shown on Step 2. Repeat this procedure for the other pair.

2. Cut four ¼" splines ⅞" wide by 24" long. Check the fit of the splines in the ¼" grooves.

3. Glue, spline, and clamp two of the plywood quarter sections together. Use the notches cut in the plywood to hold the clamps' heads as shown on Step 3 of the Assembly Sequence Drawing, alternating the clamps to equalize pressure. Be careful to keep the long edge flush. Glue and clamp the other two pieces.

4. Using a straight board as a fence, a ½" straight bit, and a backing board on the bottom to prevent routing into your workbench top, rout several shallow passes to trim 1/16" off the long edge (see Step 4 of the Assembly Sequence Drawing) to ensure a perfectly straight edge. Repeat on the other plywood section.

5. Rout a ¼" slot ½" deep along the long edge of each half section (see Step 5 of the Assembly Sequence Drawing). *continued*

SUNBURST DINING TABLE

continued

A

Clamp the two halves of the table together.

6. Glue, spline, and clamp the two halves together as shown in photo A *above*. (As you can see in the photo, our notches were not exactly the same as shown on the drawings. When gluing the panels together, we found that a few more notches would have been helpful.)

Build the solid-oak band

1. Rip and crosscut 16 pieces of ¾″ oak to 5¼ × 21″ for the upper band pieces (L) and lower band pieces (M).

2. Miter-cut the ends of each piece at a 22½° angle for a 20⅜″ finished length. (We miter-cut eight pieces of equal-length scrap and clamped them together to ensure an accurate angle setting.)

3. Glue and clamp the top band together. (We laid the pieces on waxed paper on a half sheet of particleboard and band-clamped them together. Then we clamped each band piece to the particleboard to ensure a flat band.) Later, repeat this process for the lower band.

4. Make alignment marks (see the Ring Assembly Drawing, *top right*) at the centerline of several of the upper band pieces (L). Position one band on top of the other one, aligning the marked centerlines of the top band pieces with the joint lines of the bottom band. Glue and clamp the bands to each other as shown in photo B, *opposite, top left*.

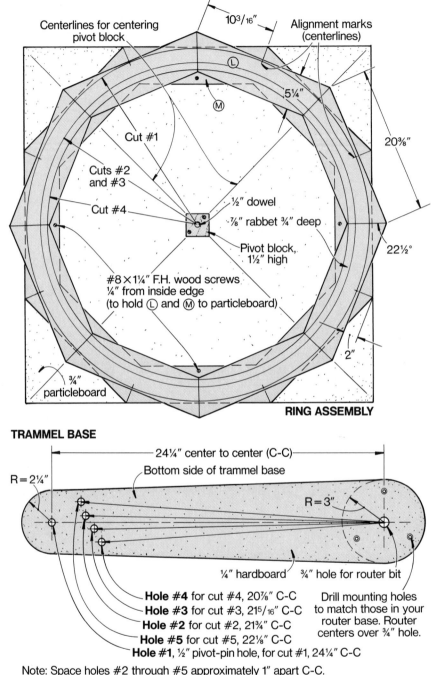

Centerlines for centering pivot block

Alignment marks (centerlines)

10³/₁₆″

Cut #1

Cuts #2 and #3

Cut #4

5¼″

20⅜″

22½°

½″ dowel

⅞″ rabbet ¾″ deep

Pivot block, 1½″ high

#8 × 1¼″ F.H. wood screws ¼″ from inside edge (to hold Ⓛ and Ⓜ to particleboard)

¾″ particleboard

2″

RING ASSEMBLY

TRAMMEL BASE

24¼″ center to center (C-C)

Bottom side of trammel base

R = 2¼″

R = 3″

¼″ hardboard   ¾″ hole for router bit

Hole #4 for cut #4, 20⅞″ C-C
Hole #3 for cut #3, 21⁵/₁₆″ C-C
Hole #2 for cut #2, 21¾″ C-C
Hole #5 for cut #5, 22⅛″ C-C
Hole #1, ½″ pivot-pin hole, for cut #1, 24¼″ C-C

Note: Space holes #2 through #5 approximately 1″ apart C-C.

Drill mounting holes to match those in your router base. Router centers over ¾″ hole.

ROUTING SEQUENCE
Note: All routing made in several passes.

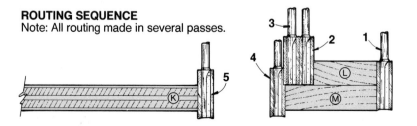

B

Apply glue, then align and clamp the two oak bands together.

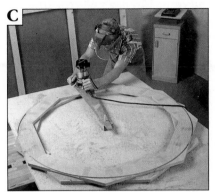

C

Mount the trammel, and rout the laminated-oak band to shape.

Build the trammel base and rout the oak band round

1. Cut the trammel base to shape, and drill the five pivot-pin holes where dimensioned on the Trammel Base Drawing, *opposite, middle*. Remove the plastic subbase from your router; mount the trammel base in its place.

2. To make the pivot block for the trammel base, cut two pieces of ¾″ scrap to 3×3″. Glue and clamp together, draw diagonals, and drill a ½″ hole through the center of the block.

3. Lay the oak bands on a piece of particleboard with the upper band on top. Then drill shank and pilot holes through the lower band pieces (M) where shown on the Ring Assembly Drawing. Screw them to the particleboard.

4. Locate and mark the center of the band on the particleboard (we used a long straightedge to draw lines between the opposite joint lines to find center). Center the hole in the pivot block directly over the centerpoint, and screw the block in position. Glue a 4″ length of ½″ dowel in the hole in the block.

5. Chuck a ½″ carbide-tipped straight bit into your router. Position pivot-pin hole #1 on the ½″ dowel in the pivot block. Rout ¼″ deep into the oak band to start forming the outside to shape as shown in photo C *above right* and on the Trammel Base and Routing Sequence drawings, *opposite*. Lower the bit about ³⁄₁₆″ per pass until you cut through the band.

6. Using trammel-base hole #2 and then #3 on the pivot block, rout the ⅞″ rabbet ¾″ deep where shown on the Trammel Base and Routing Sequence drawings. (We first checked the depth of the rabbet on a scrap piece of oak plywood.) Using hole #4, make several passes to cut through the band to form the inside circumference.

7. Remove the band from the particleboard, and rout a chamfer on the top and bottom outside edge of the oak band with a chamfer bit (as shown on the Edge Detail *below*).

8. Finally, rout or sand a slight chamfer on the bottom inside edge of the bottom band.

EDGE DETAIL

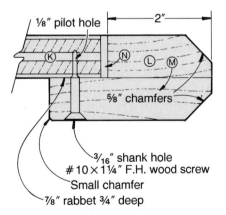

⅛″ pilot hole

2″

K

N L M

⅝″ chamfers

³⁄₁₆″ shank hole
#10 × 1¼″ F.H. wood screw
Small chamfer
⅞″ rabbet ¾″ deep

Rout the plywood top

1. Remove the pivot block from the particleboard. Lay the plywood top, good side down, on the particleboard. Drill a ½″ hole ½″ deep at the exact center of the top (where the joint lines converge). Glue a ½″ dowel 3″ long in the hole.

2. Using hole #5 in the trammel base, rout the plywood top to shape, again cutting through the ¾″ thickness in several passes. Trim the ½″ dowel so it protrudes ½″; you'll use the dowel later to center the tabletop on the base.

Assemble the table

1. Center the plywood top in the ⅞″ rabbet in the oak band. Measure the width of the gap, and cut a 10″ scrap test strip to the measured width. Crosscut the strip into four short spacers, and position the spacers in the gap around the plywood to check for a proper fit and to center the plywood. Adjust the width, if necessary, and then cut the four walnut strips (N) to 34⁹⁄₁₆″.

2. Drill shank and pilot holes to the sizes noted on the Edge Detail, and fasten the oak band to the plywood top.

3. Put glue in the gap and insert the walnut strips. For a tight fit, you may need to trim the last strip before inserting it.

4. Being *extremely careful* not to go through the veneer, plane, scrape, and sand the walnut strips flush with the plywood top.

5. Finish-sand the base and tabletop. Stain and finish.

6. Drill a ½″ hole ½″ deep in the center of the tabletop support to align the tabletop with its protruding ½″ dowel.

7. Center the tabletop on the base, and drill shank and pilot holes through the bottom of the supports into the bottom of the tabletop. Counterbore the screws. Attach the tabletop to the base, and attach the floor glides.

OAK HERRINGBONE DINING TABLE

Have you ever admired the geometric beauty of a parquet floor—and wondered how you could apply it to furniture or other woodworking projects? Here's the answer. Using our onlay technique, you can lay up panels of any size. This classic herringbone-pattern oak table is a delightful for-instance.

Form the four legs

1. Rip and crosscut 12 pieces of 1 1/16"-thick oak stock to 3 5/16 × 29" for the legs (D). With the edges and ends flush, glue and clamp three pieces together face-to-face for each of the four table legs.

2. After the glue dries, scrape off the squeeze-out, plane one laminated edge smooth, and rip the opposite edge for a 3 3/16" finished width. Now crosscut 1/4" off one end of each leg for a square end. Set a stop, and cut the opposite end so each leg measures 28" long.

3. Using a rule and straightedge, measure and mark the saw-cut layout lines on all four faces of one leg where dimensioned on the Leg Drawing *opposite, bottom, far right.*

4. Following the instructions on the Cutting the Leg Tapers Drawing, *opposite, top,* cut each leg. If you don't have a taper jig, see the Buying Guide, page 59.

5. Sand the saw marks off each tapered surface. Sand a round-over on the bottom edges of each laminated leg.

Make the apron rails and assemble the base

1. Cut the side rails (E) and end rails (F) to the sizes stated in the Bill of Materials. Cut four corner blocks (G) to size. (We cut a piece *continued*

Bill of Materials

Part	Finished Size*			Mat.	Qty.
	T	W	L		
A* substrate	3/4"	33"	70 3/4"	PB	1
B* banding	1 1/16"	3"	76 3/4"	O	2
C* banding	1 1/16"	3"	39"	O	2
D* leg	3 3/16"	3 3/16"	28"	LO	4
E side rail	1 1/16"	3"	69"	O	2
F end rail	1 1/16"	3"	31 1/4"	O	2
G* corner block	1 1/16"	3"	7"	O	4
H support rail	1 1/16"	3"	34 3/4"	O	2

*Parts marked with an * are cut larger initially, then trimmed to finished size. Please read the instructions before cutting.

Material Key: PB—particleboard, O—oak, LO—laminated oak.

Supplies: 14—1 × 1" chair-leg braces (Stanley part no. 996 1/2) and 2—#8 × 3/4" flathead wood screws per brace, #10 × 1 1/2" flathead wood screws, 4—3/8 × 4" hanger bolts with nuts and flat washers, stain, polyurethane sanding sealer, clear polyurethane, #0000 steel wool.

CUTTING THE LEG TAPERS

STEP 1. Adjust the angle of the taper jig so the saw-cut layout line on the leg runs parallel to the fence.

STEP 2. Adjust the fence position so the blade lines up with the layout line. Cut two adjacent sides on all four legs.

STEP 3. Adjust the angle of the taper jig so the remaining saw-cut layout line on the leg runs parallel to the fence.

STEP 4. Adjust the fence position so the blade lines up with the remaining layout line. Cut the other two adjacent sides on each leg.

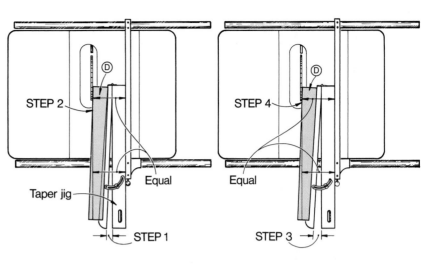

JOINING THE RAILS AND LEGS

STEP 1. Locate centerpoints. Drill a ⅜" hole for hanger bolt and use a #10 screw pilot for the screw holes.

STEP 2. Mark a corner-block reference line on both ends of Ⓔ and Ⓕ.

STEP 3. Position corner block on Ⓕ, and drill pilot holes. Glue and screw blocks to both ends of both Ⓕ's.

STEP 4. Drill pilot holes, and screw corner blocks to both ends of Ⓔ.

STEP 5. Chamfer the top of each leg.

STEP 6. Position the top of the leg flush with the top of the apron rails. Through the ⅜" hole in the corner block, drill a pilot hole into the leg. Fasten each leg to the apron assembly.

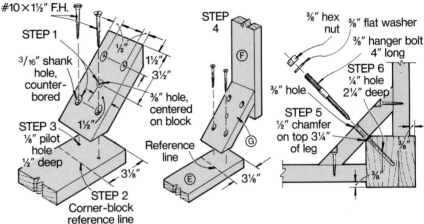

CUTAWAY VIEW

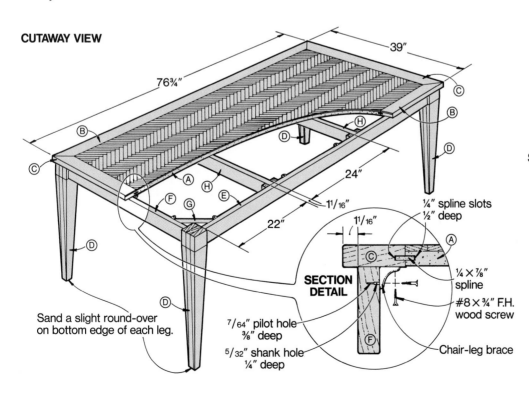

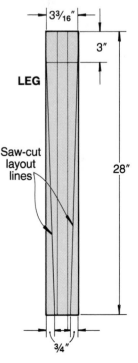

OAK HERRINGBONE DINING TABLE
continued

of 1⅟₁₆"-thick oak to 3" wide by 30" long. Then, on the tablesaw, we bevel-cut each corner block to 7" in length from the long strip.)

2. Following the steps on the Joining the Rails and Legs Drawing, page 55, join the apron rails (E, F) to the legs with the corner blocks and hanger bolts.

3. Measure the opening, and cut two support rails (H) to size. Cut eight 1⅟₁₆"-square cleats 3" long. Glue the cleats (one on each side) to the ends of the rails. Later, glue the support rails between the long apron rails (E) where dimensioned on the Cutaway View Drawing, page 55.

Rip the onlay strips

1. Start with three 6"-wide boards 8' long. Crosscut the boards into 26" lengths. (You'll end up with three 26"-long pieces and one 18"-long piece.)

2. Joint one edge of each board, and rip the boards into ¼" strips as shown in photo A, *below.* (To cut the strips, we equipped our tablesaw with a

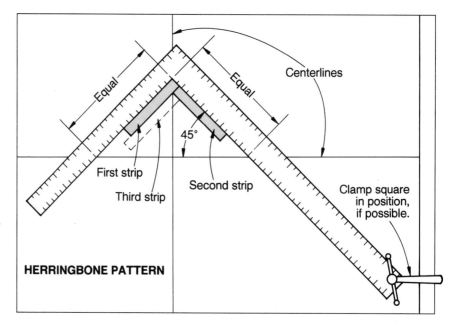

HERRINGBONE PATTERN

On the tablesaw, position the fence ¼" from the blade, and rip stock into ¼"-thick strips, using a pushstick for safety.

sharp, carbide-tipped blade. To minimize waste, we recommend a thin-kerf blade. Also, if you're using stock too short to rip safely on a tablesaw, we recommend doing it on a bandsaw. To get the straightest cut possible, use the widest bandsaw blade you have, and plane the bandsawed edge every 4 or 5 cuts.) For uniformity, rip all the strips you need (plus about 5 percent extra for waste) at the same time. If you have to come back later and reset the fence to rip additional strips, they may not come out exactly the same thickness.

3. As shown in photo B, *above right,* set a stop on your radial-arm-saw fence, and crosscut 5"-long pieces from the ¼"-thick strips. (You'll need about 800 pieces for the tabletop shown; we cut about 830 so we'd have a few extra.) Carefully check each piece for defects that may not have been apparent before ripping the board. Discard any defective pieces you come across.

To cut pieces to identical lengths, clamp a stop to the fence of your radial-arm or power miter saw.

Lay out the herringbone design

1. Cut the tabletop substrate (A) to 40" wide by 78" long.

2. Use a chalk line to bisect the substrate in both directions, forming centerlines for your pattern's layout.

3. Clamp or tape a framing square over the chalk lines where shown on the Herringbone Pattern Drawing, *top.*

Note: If it weren't for hotmelt glue sticks and glue guns, the onlay process would be impractical, if not impossible. Hotmelt glue sets up quickly so you don't need to clamp the pieces. And it's much faster and easier to use than messy contact cements or epoxies.

After a lot of testing, we decided to use Black & Decker yellow hotmelt glue because the glue has a longer working time.

4. Apply a wavy bead of hotmelt glue to the back side of the first piece. Keep the bead slightly in from the edges to prevent the glue from squeezing out from underneath the piece when you press it against the substrate (see photo C, *below*).

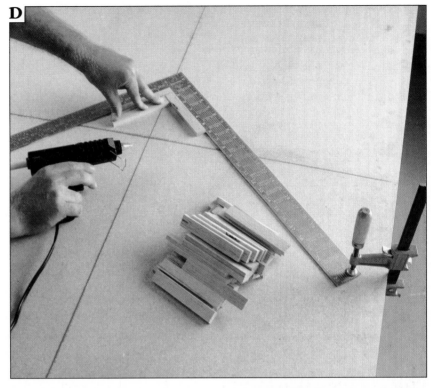

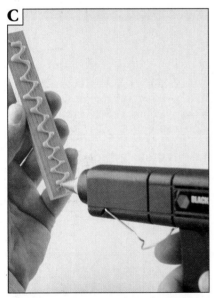

Apply a wavy line of hotmelt glue to the back of the onlay piece.

Immediately after you've applied the glue bead, press the piece down on the substrate firmly against the square. When you glue down the first two onlay pieces, you must align them precisely with the framing square and with each other. If they're slightly crooked or off-center, they'll throw off the rest of the pattern. If some of the glue does squeeze out, clean it off with a chisel before adhering the next piece.

5. Apply the next piece to the substrate and also against the framing square where shown in photo D, *above*.

Note: No matter how carefully you've cut your pieces, a few of them probably will end up a bit too long, too short, or too wide as shown in photo E, right. Or, you may glue down a piece slightly crooked. If you've accidentally glued down an ill-fitting piece, pop it off with a chisel and substitute another one.

continued

If you've glued down a too-wide strip, pop it off with a chisel and apply a new piece.

OAK HERRINGBONE DINING TABLE
continued

6. Using the first two pieces as guides, lay an initial path two strips wide. Work from the center until you reach one end of the substrate. Then go back and work in the other direction as shown in photo F, *below.* Also, when

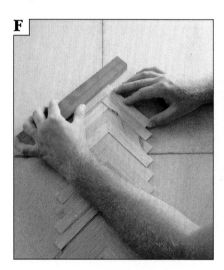

laying the onlay pieces in the direction of the arrow formed by the herringbone pattern, you'll need a straightedge (we used a wood block) to keep the pieces aligned as shown in the photo.

7. After you've glued down the center path, clamp a square to one side, as shown in photo G, *top, center.* Lay a single row of pieces on one side of the center path until you reach the other end. Continue laying single rows on both sides of the center path until you've covered the entire surface of the substrate.

Cut the panel to finished size
1. After you've glued down all the pieces, belt-sand the entire surface with 80-grit sandpaper.

2. Then, on the top surface, mark the finished size of your panel, minus the width of the edge band or trim. With a square, transfer the marks to the edges of the panel, as shown in photo H, *below.* Then flip the panel upside

Mark the panel's finished size, then transfer the marks to the back side.

down, and transfer the lines to the bottom side.

3. Cut the panel to finished size, using a portable circular saw equipped with a sharp carbide-tipped blade. For each cut, align the saw blade with the marked line, and clamp a straightedge to the workpiece to serve as a guide. See photo I, *below.*

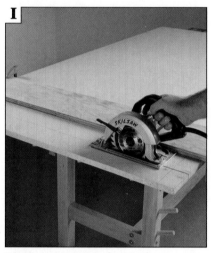

Clamp a straightedge to the workpiece, and cut the top to finished size.

Attach the edge band
Note: Onlay projects need an edge band or trim piece to cover the exposed edges of the substrate and the onlay pieces.

1. Referring to the Bill of Materials, page 54, and the Cutaway View Drawing, page 55, cut the banding pieces (B, C) to size. With a router and slot-cutting bit, rout ¼" spline slots ½" deep in the band and substrate edges as shown on the Assembled Section View Drawing *below.* Cut the splines to size.

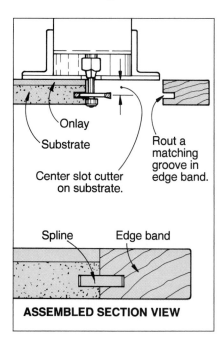

Onlay
Substrate

Rout a matching groove in edge band.

Center slot cutter on substrate.

Spline   Edge band

ASSEMBLED SECTION VIEW

2. Use woodworker's glue and pipe or bar clamps to spline the band to the panel. Later, remove the clamps and belt-sand the panel with 100-grit sandpaper.

Sand the surface and fill the gaps

If you've used all one species of wood, we suggest filling the cracks between the onlay strips with FIX pigmented wood filler after the initial belt-sanding. Force the wood filler into the cracks with a putty knife, as

We used FIX oak-colored wood patch to fill the cracks between the oak onlay strips on our tabletop. Force the wood filler into the cracks with a putty knife.

shown in photo J, *above,* and let it dry. Belt-sand the entire surface with 100-grit paper, followed by 150-grit paper. Finish-sand the entire surface with 220- and 320-grit paper.

Secure the base to the tabletop

1. Place the tabletop facedown on a workbench or sawhorses. Position the base (also upside down) on top of the tabletop. Center the base on the top, and lightly clamp it in place.

2. Using chair-leg braces, secure the base to the tabletop (see the Section Detail accompanying the Cutaway View Drawing, page 55, for hole and screw sizes). We used four braces along each side and three across each end.

Add the finish

1. With the table still facedown, sand a round-over on the bottom edges of the apron rails and on the corners of the legs. Finish-sand the legs and

apron rails. Turn the assembled table right side up, and finish-sand the tabletop and edges.

2. Apply the stain of your choice. Apply polyurethane sanding sealer to the assembly. Follow with several coats of clear polyurethane.

Buying Guide

• **Taper jig.** An extruded aluminum jig, 23" long, for right- and left-handed use, catalog no. 43471. To obtain the current price, contact The Woodworkers' Store, 21801 Industrial Blvd., Rogers, MN 55374-9514. Or call 612/428-2199.

RAISED-PANEL LIBRARY DESK

Distinctive raised-panel pedestals and a nicely tailored oak and plastic-laminate tabletop combine to make this traditional library desk a woodworking project of extraordinary merit.

Build the top

1. Cut the plywood center panel (A) and the two plywood side panels (B) to finished size.

2. Cut the plastic laminates (C, D) and balance sheets (E, F) to size plus 1″ longer and 1″ wider.

3. Apply two coats of contact cement to the top of the plywood center panel (A) and to the back side of the center plastic laminate (C); let dry between coats. Then apply the laminate. (You may want to enlist a helper when you position the laminate on the plywood to ensure that it overlaps the plywood on all sides.) Trim the overlap using a router fitted with a flush-cutting laminate trimmer.

4. Glue the balance sheet (E) to the bottom of the plywood, then trim it as you did with the plastic laminate. (The balance sheet stabilizes the panel and reduces the chances of it warping.) Apply the laminate and balance sheet to the side panels (B), then trim away the excess.

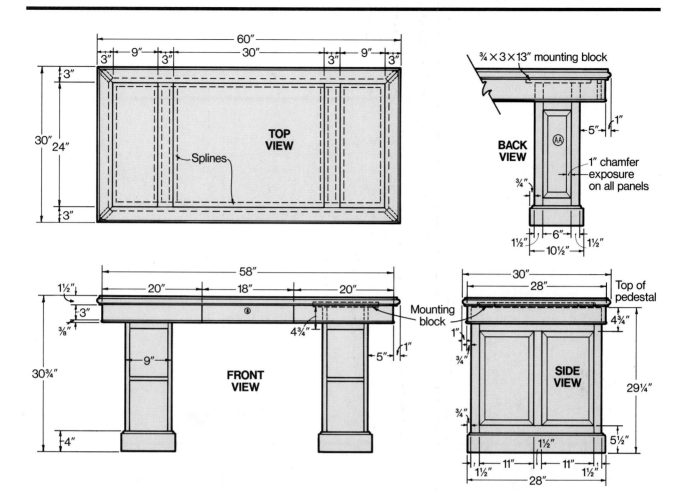

TOP VIEW

Splines

60″
3″ 9″ 3″ 30″ 3″ 9″ 3″
30″ 24″
3″
3″

¾ × 3 × 13″ mounting block

BACK VIEW

AA

5″ 1″
¾″
1″ chamfer exposure on all panels
1½″ 6″ 1½″
10½″

FRONT VIEW

58″
1½″ 20″ 18″ 20″
3″
⅜″
9″
30¾″
4″
4¾″
Mounting block
5″ 1″

SIDE VIEW

30″
28″ Top of pedestal
4¾″
1″
¾″
¾″
29¼″
¾″
1½″ 5½″
11″ 11″
1½″ 1½″
28″

5. Rip the front and back rails (G) and the end rails (H), then crosscut to length plus 1″. Cut the panel divider pieces (I) to size.

6. Using either a tablesaw fitted with a dado blade or a router and a slotting cutter, cut ¼″ grooves ½″ deep, centered, along all four edges of the three laminated panels and the dividers (I). Also cut like-size grooves along the inside edges of the red oak rails (G, H). (It's vital when cutting the grooves to keep the tops of the pieces against the tablesaw fence, or against the base of the router, to ensure that the grooves line up. Otherwise, you may end up with pieces that don't fit together flush on the top side. Cut scrap material to experiment, if necessary.)

7. Cut ¼″ hardboard splines ¹⁵⁄₁₆″ wide for all spline grooves. Dry-clamp the three panels and dividers together, checking that all edges are flush. Dry-clamp the

front and back rails (G) to the assembly, and mark the location of the miter joints. Cut the miters on the ends of both G pieces. Reclamp the mitered front and back rails to the assembly. Now position the end rails (H) under the assembly and along the ends, mark the position of the miters, and cut to size.

Cut the stopped-spline groove along the miter joints (we measured the stop mark and used a router to cut the stopped-spline groove as shown in photo A, *right*), then cut the hardboard splines to fit the miter joints. Dry-clamp the rails (G, H) in place to check the fit of all the joints, and check that all the pieces fit flush across the top.

8. Remove the clamps and glue the splines in the grooves in the panels, then glue and position the dividers between the panels.

A

Tenon-spline joinery fortifies an otherwise weak miter joint.

Apply glue in the grooves and to the rails, install the splines in the mitered ends, and clamp the rails (G, H) to the assembly.

9. After the glue forms a tough skin, remove any excess. When the glue is thoroughly dry, remove the clamps and any remaining glue. Using a ½″ round-over bit, rout a bead on the top and bottom edges of the rails as shown   *continued*

RAISED-PANEL LIBRARY DESK
continued

EXPLODED VIEW

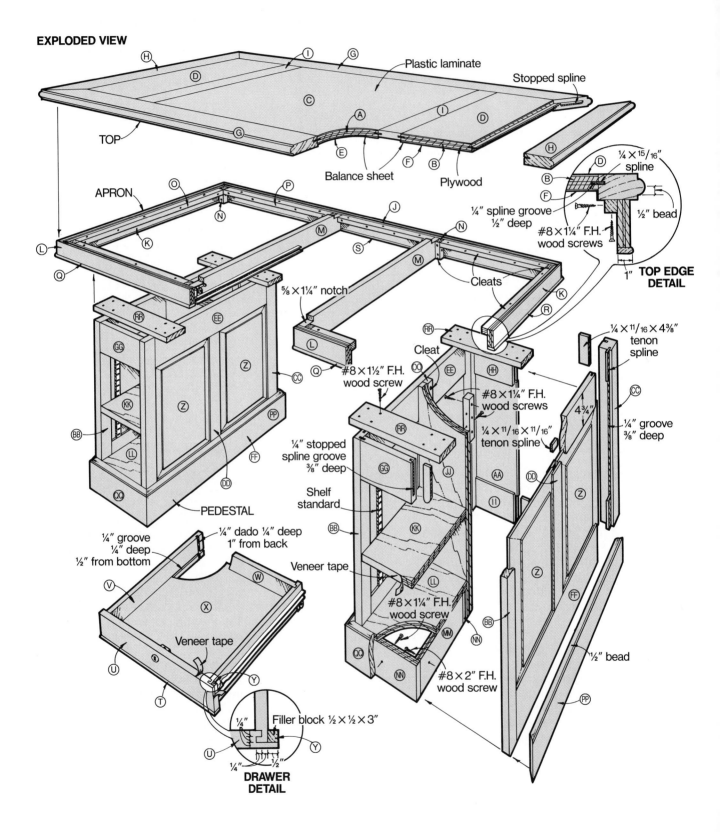

Plastic laminate

Stopped spline

TOP

Balance sheet

Plywood

APRON

⅝ × 1¼" notch

Cleats

¼ × ¹⁵/₁₆"
spline

¼" spline groove
½" deep

½" bead

#8 × 1¼" F.H.
wood screws

1"

**TOP EDGE
DETAIL**

Cleat

¼ × ¹¹/₁₆ × 4⅜"
tenon
spline

4¾"

¼" groove
⅜" deep

#8 × 1½" F.H.
wood screw

¼" stopped
spline groove
⅜" deep

Shelf
standard

#8 × 1¼" F.H.
wood screws

¼ × ¹¹/₁₆ × ¹¹/₁₆"
tenon spline

PEDESTAL

¼" groove
¼" deep
½" from bottom

¼" dado ¼" deep
1" from back

Veneer tape

Veneer tape

#8 × 1¼" F.H.
wood screw

#8 × 2" F.H.
wood screw

½" bead

Filler block ½ × ½ × 3"

¼"

¼"   ½"

**DRAWER
DETAIL**

Bill of Materials

Part	T	W	L	Mat.	Qty.
Top					
A center panel	¾"	24"	30"	FP	1
B side panel	¾"	9"	24"	FP	2
C* center laminate	1/16"	24"	30"	PL	1
D* side laminate	1/16"	9"	24"	PL	2
E* balance sheet	1/16"	24"	30"	BS	1
F* balance sheet	1/16"	9"	24"	BS	2
G* front/back rail	1½"	3"	60"	RO	2
H* end rail	1½"	3"	30"	RO	2
I divider	¾"	3"	24"	RO	2
Apron Assembly					
J back apron	¾"	3"	58"	ROP	1
K end apron	¾"	3"	28"	ROP	2
L front apron	¾"	3"	20"	ROP	2
M guide rail	¾"	3⅝"	26½"	FP	2
N cleat	¾"	¾"	3"	P	8
O cleat	¾"	¾"	25"	P	2
P cleat	¾"	¾"	18"	P	1
Q* front trim	⅜"	1"	20¼"	O	2
R* end trim	⅜"	1"	28½"	O	2
S* back trim	⅜"	1"	58½"	O	1
Drawer					
T* front bottom	⅜"	1"	17¾"	O	1
U* front	¾"	3"	17¾"	ROP	1
V side	½"	3"	17⅞"	O	2
W back	½"	2¼"	16¼"	O	1
X bottom	¼"	17⅝"	16¼"	ROP	1
Y filler block	½"	½"	3"	O	2
Pedestals					
Z* raised panel	½"	11¹¹/₁₆"	19⁹/₁₆"	O	8
AA* end panel	½"	6¹¹/₁₆"	19⁹/₁₆"	O	2
BB front stile	¾"	1½"	29⅛"	O	4
CC rear stile	1½"	1½"	29⅛"	O	4
DD mullion	¾"	1½"	18⅞"	O	4
EE top rail	¾"	4¾"	23½"	O	4
FF bottom rail	¾"	5½"	23½"	O	4
GG front rail	¾"	4¾"	7½"	O	2
HH back top rail	¾"	4¾"	6"	O	2
II back bottom rail	¾"	5½"	6"	O	2
JJ center divider	¾"	7½"	29⅛"	ROP	2
KK adjust. shelf	¾"	12⅜"	7⅜"	ROP	2
LL bottom shelf	¾"	12½"	7½"	ROP	2
MM base	¾"	3¼"	11"	FP	4
NN base	¾"	3¼"	7½"	FP	4
OO cleat	¾"	¾"	4¾"	O	4
PP* base molding	¾"	4"	28"	O	4
QQ* base molding	¾"	4"	10½"	O	4
RR mounting block	¾"	3"	13"	O	4

*Parts marked with an * are cut larger initially, then trimmed to finished size. Please read the instructions before cutting.

Material Key: FP—fir plywood, PL—plastic laminate, BS—balance sheet, RO—red oak, ROP—red oak plywood, P—pine, O—oak.
Supplies: white glue, ¼" hardboard for splines, Knape Vogt 1300—16" drawer slides, drawer lock, brads, shelf standards, #8×1¼" flathead wood screws, #8×1½" flathead wood screws, #8×2" flathead wood screws, stain, polyurethane.

Cutting List
1 Piece—¾×48×96" Fir Plywood
1 Piece—30×72" Plastic Laminate
1 Piece—30×72" Balance Sheet
5 Pieces—¾×7¼×96" Red Oak
1 Piece—1½×7¼×96" Red Oak
1 Piece—1½×7¼×36" Red Oak
3 Pieces—½×9¼×96" Red Oak
1 Piece—¼×24×24" Red Oak Plywood
1 Piece—¾×48×96" Red Oak Plywood
1 Piece—¾×7¼×48" Pine

in the Top Edge Detail, *opposite.* Sand the top assembly, being careful not to sand the laminate.

Build the apron assembly

1. Rip, then crosscut the back apron (J) and the end aprons (K) to size plus 1" in length. Rip a piece of oak plywood to 3", and crosscut it to 60". Now, cut one 21"-long piece from each end. (These two end pieces are the front aprons [L]. Set aside the remaining middle piece; you'll use it later as the drawer front [U]. This ensures a continuous flow of wood grain across the front aprons and drawer.)

Miter both ends of the back and end aprons, and one end of each of the front aprons. Cut the drawer guide rails (M) to size, then cut ⅝×1¼" notches in each end of both rails.

2. Cut the pine cleats (N, O, P) to size. Drill pilot holes through the cleats for mounting them to the underside of the top and to the aprons.

3. Using #8×1¼" wood screws, fasten the corner cleats (N) to the inside corners of the mitered joints, and at the same time glue the apron miters together. Glue and screw cleats (O, P) to the aprons. Finally, mount the drawer guide rails (M) to the assembly.

4. Flip the top upside down, then center the apron on the top. The top should overhang the apron 1" on all sides. Fasten the apron assembly to the underside of the top.

5. Cut the front trim pieces (Q), the end trim pieces (R), the back trim piece (S), and the drawer front bottom piece (T) to size plus 1" in length. (To obtain the ⅜" stock, we ripped ¾" thick oak to 1" width. Then, using a feather board and a pushstick, we resawed the pieces on the tablesaw, ending up with pieces measuring ⅜×1".)

Form the round-overs along one edge of all the trim pieces with a ³/₁₆" round-over bit. (We cut ours on a router table with a fence.) Miter the *continued*

RAISED-PANEL LIBRARY DESK
continued

ends, then glue and brad into position on the bottom of the aprons. Set the drawer front bottom (T) aside for now.

6. Attach the drawer slides to the guide rails (M) as shown in photo B *below.* Sand the entire assembly smooth.

Mount the drawer slides flush with the bottom of the guide rails.

Build the drawer

1. Crosscut the previously cut drawer front (U) (cut in step 1 of "Build the apron assembly") to length. Then rip and crosscut the drawer sides (V), back (W), and bottom (X) to size.

2. Cut a ¼" groove ¼" deep and ½" up from the bottom along pieces U and V as shown on the Drawer Detail accompanying the Exploded View Drawing, page 62. Cut a ¼" dado ¼" deep and 1" from the back on the drawer sides (V). On the front ends of the sides, cut a ¼" dado ¼" deep and ¼" from the front (see the Drawer Detail).

3. Using a pushblock or tenon jig, push the drawer front through the tablesaw to cut a ¼" dado 1" deep on both ends. Trim one of the tongues on each end so it's only ¼" long. Also, cut the filler blocks (Y) to size.

4. Dry-clamp the drawer parts and check the fit. Glue and clamp the drawer together. After the glue dries, remove the clamps, sand the drawer smooth, and apply oak veneer tape where shown on the Exploded View

Drawing. Install the lock in the drawer front. Cut front bottom piece T to length, then glue and brad it to the bottom of the drawer front.

Cut the stiles, rails, and panels

1. Rip oak stock for the eight raised panels (Z) and two end panels (AA). (We used ½" oak stock for the raised panels. You can either resaw or plane thicker stock to size or special-order it through your local lumberyard or a mail-order source. When ripping the stock for panels, we tried to keep the pieces under 4" wide for a more stable finished panel. We cut each piece to length plus 1" and to width plus ¼". The finished size of each panel is listed in the Bill of Materials, page 63.)

2. Lay out each panel and match the pieces together for uniform grain pattern and color. Mark each panel for ease in assembling later. When laying out the panels, check the mating surfaces between the boards and joints, if necessary.

3. Glue and clamp each panel together, being sure that the pieces used to make up the panel lie flat on the clamps (this helps ensure a flat panel).

4. Cut the front stiles (BB), rear stiles (CC), mullions (DD), top rails (EE), and bottom rails (FF) to size. Now cut the front rails (GG), back top rails (HH), and back bottom rails (II) to size.

5. Cut a ¼" stopped groove ⅜" deep and 4" long along the top edges of BBs and both ends of GGs. Cut ¼" grooves ⅜" deep along the edges and ends of DDs, and along one edge and both ends of EEs, FFs, HHs, and IIs. Cut a ¼" groove ⅜" deep and ¼" back from the face on two edges of CCs. Cut ¼" hardboard splines for the spline-groove joints.

6. Cut the panels to size.

Raise the panels

1. Fasten an auxiliary wooden fence to your tablesaw fence for added stability when making the cuts in step 3 below. (Our auxiliary fence measured 6" high.)

2. Position the fence 1⅜" from the outside edge of the tablesaw blade. As shown in photo C, *below,* make ⅛" deep cuts 1⅜" in from the outside edges of each panel to form the shoulder.

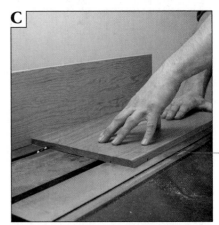

The panel-raising sequence begins when you make shoulder cuts along the edges of each of the glued-up panels.

3. Using the dimensions on the Panel Section Detail, *below,* mark a 7° reference line from one edge of the panel to the bottom of the shoulder cut. (The mark shows up in photo D, *opposite, top left.*)

Note: As shown in the photos, we have a zero-clearance insert in place for these cuts. The insert eliminates the possibility of the

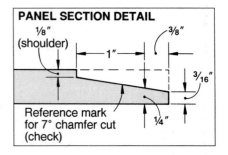

PANEL SECTION DETAIL
⅛" (shoulder) · ⅜· 1" · ³⁄₁₆" · ¼"
Reference mark for 7° chamfer cut (check)

D

Position the rip fence.

panel getting hung up on its way through the blade.

4. Tilt your tablesaw blade 7° from vertical, and raise the blade 1⅜″ above the surface of the saw table. Position the fence 3⁄16″ from the inside edge of the blade where shown in photo D. Align the blade with the marked reference line. (Since it's almost impossible to measure a saw blade's bevel to within 1°, we cranked the blade to an angle and height that looked about right. Then we eyeballed both of them as shown in photo E, *below.*) Run some scrap material through the saw, then fine-tune both the

E

Eyeball the angle and height of the cut. Then, using scrap material, fine-tune your guess.

angle and height until you're right on the money.

5. Make the chamfer cuts to form the cheeks as shown in photo F, *below.*

F

A wide auxiliary fence helps stabilize the panel.

6. After making all the chamfer cuts, dry-clamp each assembly together to check the fit of the panels in the openings. Then cut 1⁄16″ from the width and length of each panel to allow it to move freely in the frame grooves. The panels must fit a bit loose to allow them to expand later without splitting the frames.

7. Sand the panels and cheeks smooth. (We wrapped sandpaper around a wood block to sand the saw marks from the cheeks.) When sanding, do so carefully so you don't round over the edges where the pieces join.

Build the pedestals

1. Dry-clamp the stiles (BB, CC), mullions (DD), rails (EE, FF), hardboard splines, and panels (Z) together, and check the fit. Adjust, if necessary, then glue and clamp the four pedestal side assemblies together, being sure to check that they are perfectly square.

2. After the glue has dried, remove the clamps and excess glue. Now dry-clamp the side assemblies together, using parts AA, GG, HH, and II. Check for square with a try square.

3. Cut the center dividers (JJ), adjustable shelves (KK), bottom shelves (LL), and base pieces (MM, NN) to size. Check the fit of the dividers, adjustable shelves, bottom shelves, and base pieces in the dry-clamped pedestals. All pieces (except for the adjustable shelf, which floats) should fit snugly without forcing the pedestal assembly out of square.

4. Glue and nail base pieces MM and NN together.

5. Remove the clamps, then glue the side assemblies together using the hardboard splines, rails (GG, HH, II), end panels (AA), and base assembly (MM, NN). Reclamp and check for square.

6. After the glue has dried, remove the clamps and excess glue. Cut the cleats (OO) to size, then drill pilot holes through the cleats for mounting to the dividers (JJ) and the top rails (EE). Using #8 × 1¼″ wood screws, fasten the cleats to the dividers. Install the dividers between the side assemblies and screw to the sides of the top rails and to the back of NN.

7. Cut base molding pieces (PP, QQ) to size plus 1″ in length. Using a router fitted with a ½″ round-over bit, rout the decorative edge on the pieces. Miter each end of each piece to fit around each pedestal. Screw the molding pieces to the base from the inside of the base assembly (see the Exploded View Drawing, page 62).

Finish and assemble

1. Finish-sand the top, drawer, and pedestals. Carefully mask off the laminate, then stain, if desired, and apply finish (we used satin polyurethane).

2. Fasten the shelf standards to the back side of the raised panels (Z), then attach the drawer slides to the sides of the drawer.

3. Cut the mounting blocks (RR) to size and fasten to the top of each pedestal. With the top upside down on a blanket to prevent it from being scratched, position the pedestals and screw them to the top.

OUTDOOR FURNITURE

Pull up a settee, gather 'round our redwood table, build a planter or two or three, turn out a set of our teak director's chairs, or relax on a sturdy mahogany garden bench. These five projects can make summertime living at your house a lot easier.

SOLID-OAK SETTEE

Luis Elizondo, a *WOOD®* magazine reader from Texas, sent us the plan for this sweetheart of a settee. We were so impressed with his design, we decided to share it with our readers. First, of course, we built a prototype—two of them, actually—to verify the patterns, dimensions, and joinery. They both turned out beautifully, as you can see from the one in the photo, *opposite*. Come on, dive into this project—you'll be glad you did.

Note: For your convenience, we've listed a source on page 71 for the full-sized patterns for the settee. Or, if you just can't wait to get started, enlarge the gridded patterns on pages 70 and 71.

How we chose the wood and fasteners for our settee

After weighing the merits of several types of lumber for this project, we selected white oak. Native to the eastern United States and Canada, white oak rates as one of the heaviest, strongest, and hardest of all the oaks. The pores of this species contain tyloses—bubblelike structures that form in the vessels of certain hardwoods and resist penetration by liquids. This attribute makes white oak a perfect material for liquid containers and barrels, and an excellent candidate for our settee. If you have trouble locating white oak, or you wish to cut costs, you could substitute fir or pine pressure-treated deck material. You'll need to plane the pressure-treated stock to the thicknesses listed in the Bill of Materials, page 69.

What's the best fastener to use in this case? We recommend either stainless-steel or galvanized deck and machine screws. The tannic acid in white oak, as well as Mother Nature, causes ordinary screws to rust and stain the wood.

Enlarge the patterns and make the templates

1. To enlarge the gridded patterns, draw 1″ grids on large pieces of paper to match the 13 patterns on pages 70 and 71. Using the gridded patterns as guides, lay out the shapes of parts on the gridded paper. To do this, mark the points where the pattern outline crosses each grid line. Draw lines to connect the points. Mark the screw-hole centerpoints and reference lines on each pattern.

2. Coat the back face of each pattern with spray-on adhesive. With a helper, start at one end and work to the other, laying the patterns flat onto 1/8″ or 1/4″ hardboard. Keep the patterns as flat as possible and be sure to flatten any air bubbles.

3. Bandsaw each template to shape, cutting just *outside* the marked line. Then sand to the line for the finished shape. Don't forget to bandsaw the notches in the center-support templates (E).

4. Drill 1/8″ holes through the templates at each marked centerpoint.

5. Position the templates (except for the decorative centerpiece [P]) and trace their outlines and hole centerpoints onto the stock. See the Cutting Diagram, page 69, for reference and layout.

Machine the parts and construct the seat frame

1. Cut the seat rails (A, B) and legs (C) to the sizes listed in the Bill of Materials.

2. Bandsaw the end supports (D), center supports (E), and armrest supports (F) to the shapes traced from the templates.

3. Cut notches in the front rail (B) where shown on the Seat Frame Drawing, page 68. (We cut ours on the radial-arm saw.)

4. Rout a 1/4″ round-over along the edges of the pieces where shown on the Seat Frame Drawing. Do not round over the seat rails (A, B), center supports (E), or the top ends of the leg pieces (C, F). Sand the seat-frame members (A through F) smooth.

5. Clamp together the seat members (A, B, E), checking for square. Drill and counterbore the mounting holes, and fasten the parts together with stainless-steel or galvanized deck screws.

6. Using bar clamps, clamp the end supports (D) to the seat assembly (A, B, E). Drill the counterbores (holes for the plugs) in the end supports where marked. Then drill a 1/8″ pilot hole through the middle of the counterbore and 1¾″ into the ends of the seat rails (A, B). Enlarge the pilot holes in the end supports to $3/16$″ to form shank holes for the screws. See the Screw Hole Detail accompanying the Seat Frame Drawing, page 68, for reference. Fasten the end supports to the rails.

7. Drill the holes, and screw one armrest support (F) to each leg (C). Plug the holes in parts C and D as described in step 1 of the section "Plug the screw-hole counterbores," page 68.

8. Now drill the 1/4″ holes, and fasten each leg to the seat assembly with a stainless-steel 1/4 × 2½″ machine screw. Set the seat-frame assembly on a flat surface, check that the front legs are square with the floor, and add the two wood screws to fasten each leg to its mating end support. *continued*

SOLID-OAK SETTEE
continued

Plug the screw-hole counterbores

1. As you work, you'll need to plug the screw-hole counterbores. If you wait until you're done building the project, several of the holes are impossible to get at. To plug the holes, cut ⅜"- and ½"-diameter plugs from oak stock. (We used a plug cutter and took the time to closely match the plug grain with each settee part.)

2. Glue the plugs into the counterbores, with the grain of the plug going in the same direction as the grain of the piece being plugged (we used woodworker's glue).

Move on to the rear support and slats

1. Bandsaw the rear support (G) to shape. Transfer the reference line from the template to the top back edge of the support. Rout a ¼" round-over along the edges of the support. Cut a 1¹⁄₁₆" dado ⁵⁄₁₆" deep on each end of the support.

2. With the front edge of G ¼" ahead of the front face of A, clamp the rear support in position. See the Section View Drawing accompanying the Seat Back Assembly Drawing, page 72, for reference.

3. Drill mounting holes, and fasten the rear support to the seat frame.

4. Cut the 14 seat slats (H) to size. Rout a ¼" round-over along all edges of each slat. Drill and counterbore the mounting holes in each slat. See the Seat Slat Detail accompanying the Seat Slat Assembly Drawing, *lower right,* for hole locations.

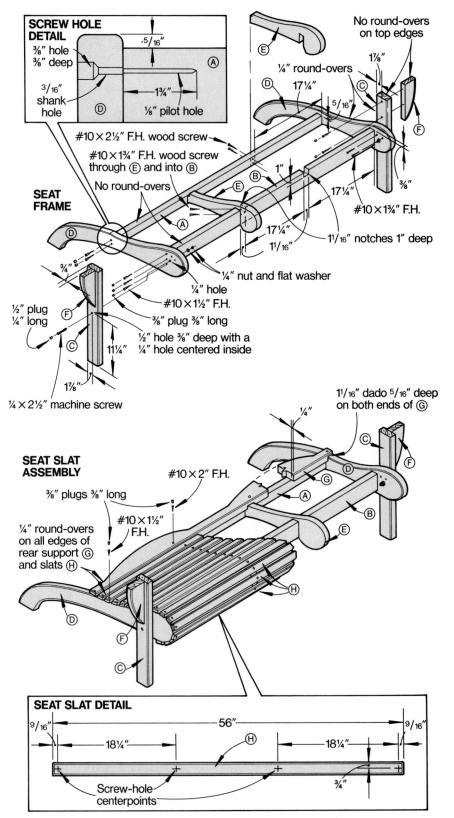

SCREW HOLE DETAIL
⅜" hole ⅜" deep
.5/16"
3/16" shank hole
1¾"
⅛" pilot hole

#10 × 2½" F.H. wood screw
#10 × 1¾" F.H. wood screw through Ⓔ and into Ⓑ
No round-overs

SEAT FRAME

No round-overs on top edges
¼" round-overs
1⅛"
17¼"
5/16"
1"
17¼"
¾"
#10 × 1¾" F.H.
17¼"
1¹⁄₁₆" notches 1" deep
1¹⁄₁₆"
¼" nut and flat washer
¼" hole
#10 × 1½" F.H.
⅜" plug ⅜" long
½" hole ⅜" deep with a ¼" hole centered inside

¾"
½" plug ¼" long
11¼"
1⅞"
¼ × 2½" machine screw

1¹⁄₁₆" dado ⁵⁄₁₆" deep on both ends of Ⓖ

SEAT SLAT ASSEMBLY
¼"
#10 × 2" F.H.
⅜" plugs ⅜" long
#10 × 1½" F.H.
¼" round-overs on all edges of rear support Ⓖ and slats Ⓗ

SEAT SLAT DETAIL
9/16"
56"
9/16"
18¼"
Ⓗ
18¼"
Screw-hole centerpoints
¾"

Cutting Diagram

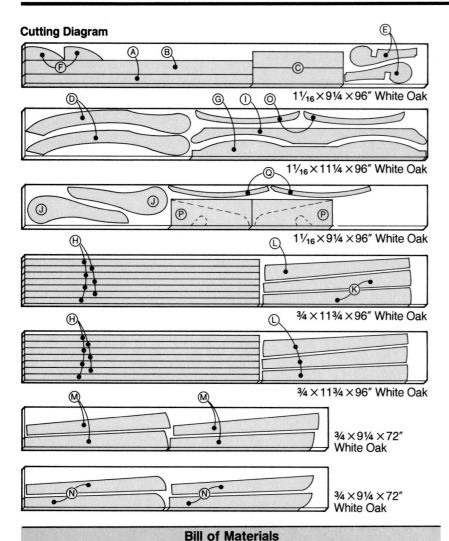

1¹⁄₁₆ × 9¼ × 96″ White Oak

1¹⁄₁₆ × 11¼ × 96″ White Oak

1¹⁄₁₆ × 9¼ × 96″ White Oak

¾ × 11¾ × 96″ White Oak

¾ × 11¾ × 96″ White Oak

¾ × 9¼ × 72″ White Oak

¾ × 9¼ × 72″ White Oak

5. Cut the pieces and build four ¼″ spacers and four ⅜″ spacers like those shown in the drawing *below.*

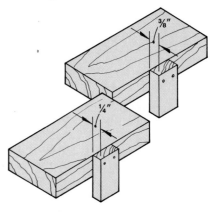

6. Position the ⅜″ spacers between the rear support (G) and the first seat slat where shown in photo A, *below.* Now, as shown, screw the seat slat to the end and center supports (D, E). Repeat the process with the ⅜″ spacers to space and fasten the next seven slats to the seat frame. Then switch to the ¼″ spacers for the four slats that go around the curve. Finally, switch back to the ⅜″ spacers to add the last two slats to the frame. *continued*

With the spacers in place, clamp a seat slat to the rear support, and screw the slat to the supports.

Bill of Materials

Part	Grid Size*			Mat.	Qty.
	T	W	L		
Seat Frame					
A rear rail	1¹⁄₁₆″	2⅛″	53⅞″	WO	1
B front rail	1¹⁄₁₆″	3¼″	53⅞″	WO	1
C leg	1¹⁄₁₆″	3¾″	21¼″	WO	2
D* end support	1¹⁄₁₆″	6″	40″	WO	2
E* center support	1¹⁄₁₆″	6″	17″	WO	2
F* armrest support	1¹⁄₁₆″	3″	10″	WO	2
Slat Supports and Slats					
G* rear support	1¹⁄₁₆″	4″	56″	WO	1
H seat slat	¾″	1½″	56″	WO	14
Seat-Back Assembly					
I* rear-slat support	1¹⁄₁₆″	4″	56″	WO	1
J* armrest	1¹⁄₁₆″	7″	25″	WO	2
K* slat	¾″	4″	36″	WO	2

Part	Grid Size*			Mat.	Qty.
	T	W	L		
L* slat	¾″	4″	36″	WO	4
M* slat	¾″	4″	35″	WO	4
N* slat	¾″	4″	34″	WO	4
O* upper-slat supp.	1¹⁄₁₆″	3″	26″	WO	2
P* center-piece	1¹⁄₁₆″	12″	20″	EW	1
Q* brace	1¹⁄₁₆″	3″	25″	WO	2

*Parts A, B, C, and H are cut to the sizes listed above. The dimensions of the remaining parts (marked with an *) are the sizes of the 1″ grid pattern for each.

Material Key: WO—white oak, EW—edge-joined white oak.
Supplies: spray adhesive; ⅛″ or ¼″ hardboard; flathead wood screws (stainless-steel or galvanized deck screws) in the following sizes: # 10 × 1″, # 10 × 1½″, , # 10 × 1¾″, # 10 × 2″, # 10 × 2½″; ¼ × 2½″ machine screw with flat washer and nut (stainless steel or brass); ¼ × 1½″ machine screw and nut; clear finish.

SOLID-OAK SETTEE
continued

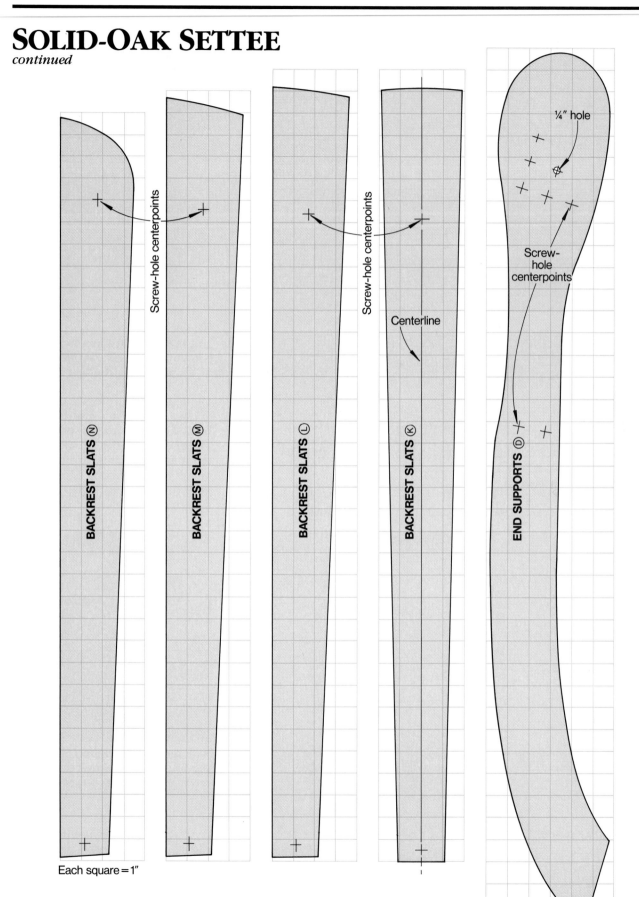

Screw-hole centerpoints

Screw-hole centerpoints

¼" hole

Screw-hole centerpoints

Centerline

BACKREST SLATS N

BACKREST SLATS M

BACKREST SLATS L

BACKREST SLATS K

END SUPPORTS D

Each square = 1"

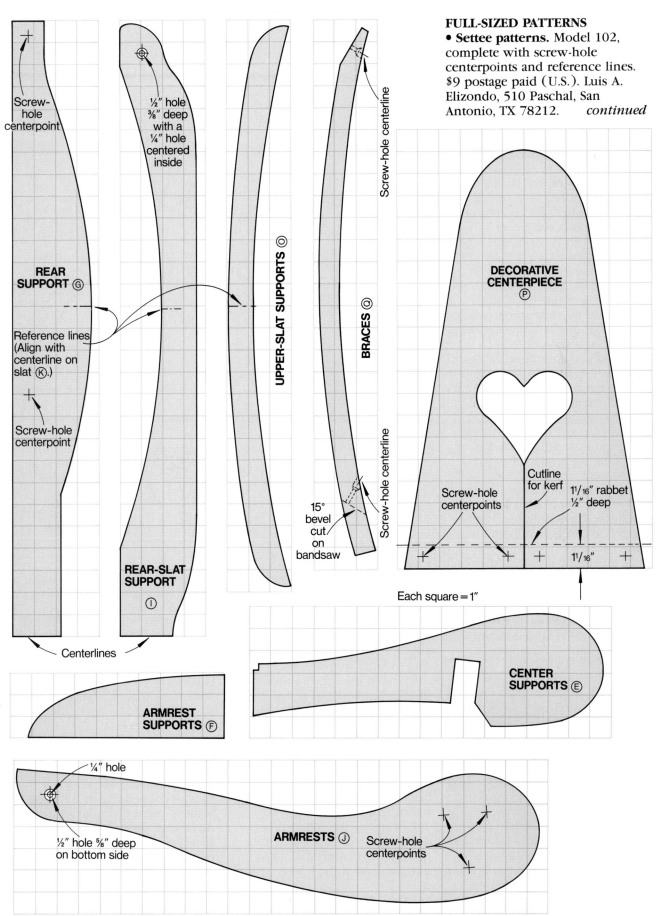

Screw-hole centerpoint

½" hole ⅜" deep with a ¼" hole centered inside

REAR SUPPORT Ⓖ

Reference lines (Align with centerline on slat Ⓚ.)

Screw-hole centerpoint

UPPER-SLAT SUPPORTS Ⓞ

BRACES Ⓠ

Screw-hole centerline

Screw-hole centerline

Screw-hole centerline

15° bevel cut on bandsaw

REAR-SLAT SUPPORT Ⓘ

Centerlines

ARMREST SUPPORTS Ⓕ

¼" hole

½" hole ⅝" deep on bottom side

ARMRESTS Ⓙ

Screw-hole centerpoints

FULL-SIZED PATTERNS
• **Settee patterns.** Model 102, complete with screw-hole centerpoints and reference lines. $9 postage paid (U.S.). Luis A. Elizondo, 510 Paschal, San Antonio, TX 78212. *continued*

DECORATIVE CENTERPIECE Ⓟ

Screw-hole centerpoints

Cutline for kerf

1¹/₁₆" rabbet ½" deep

1¹/₁₆"

Each square = 1"

CENTER SUPPORTS Ⓔ

SOLID-OAK SETTEE
continued

Add the contoured seat-back assembly

1. Cut the rear-slat support (I) and the armrests (J) to shape. Transfer the reference line from the template to the top surface of the rear-slat support. Rout a ¼" round-over along all edges of each (I, J). Drill the mounting holes, and bolt the pieces together with ¼ × 1½" machine screws and nuts.

2. Using just one screw per armrest, fasten the armrests to the armrest supports (F). (Later, you'll add two screws per arm.)

3. To get the bottom edges of the backrest slats flush, cut a temporary support from ¾"-thick stock to 3" wide by 52½" long. Fasten the support to the bottom of the rear support (G) where shown on the Section View Drawing at *right*.

4. Bandsaw the seat-back slats (K, L, M, N) to shape from ¾" stock. Mark the screw-hole centerpoints on the slats. Rout a ¼" round-over along all edges of each slat. Transfer the centerline onto both surfaces of both middle slats (K).

5. Position the middle slats (K) on the temporary spacer with the centerline on the middle slats aligned with the reference lines on the rear support (G) and rear-slat support (I) where shown in photo B, *below*. Clamp the

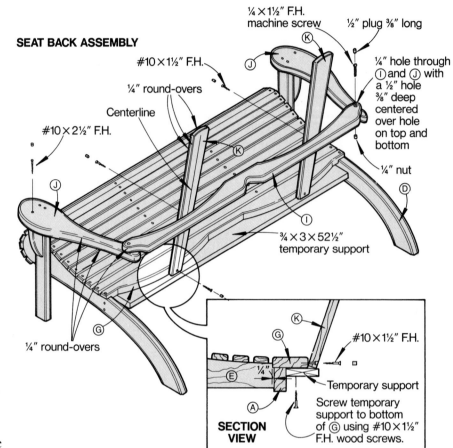

SEAT BACK ASSEMBLY

¼ × 1½" F.H. machine screw
½" plug ⅜" long
#10 × 1½" F.H.
¼" round-overs
Centerline
#10 × 2½" F.H.
¼" hole through ⓘ and ⓙ with a ½" hole ⅜" deep centered over hole on top and bottom
¼" nut
Ⓓ
Ⓙ
Ⓚ
¾ × 3 × 52½" temporary support
Ⓘ
¼" round-overs
Ⓖ

SECTION VIEW
Ⓚ
Ⓖ
#10 × 1½" F.H.
Ⓔ
¼"
Temporary support
Ⓐ
Screw temporary support to bottom of Ⓖ using #10 × 1½" F.H. wood screws.

Align the top and bottom supports, position the center slats, and fasten them to the supports.

middle slat in position, and check that the marked screw-hole centerpoints center over the rear-slat support. Drill the mounting holes. Refer to the Section View Drawing before drilling the angled hole through the slat and into the rear support.

6. Fasten the center slats (K) to the rear support and rear-slat support. When fastening each backrest slat, drive the bottom screw partway and then drive the top screw partway; continue until each screw is snug. For ease in attaching the slats, do not insert one screw all the way before inserting the other.

7. With the assembly square, drive the remaining two screws through each armrest (J), and into the tops of the legs.

8. Using the ⅜" spacers, position the backrest slats, drill the mounting holes, and fasten the slats to the settee frame.

9. Cut the upper-slat supports (O) to shape, and rout a ¼" round-over along their edges. Center and clamp one upper-slat support in place against the seat-back slats. Drill the holes and screw the support to the slats. Plug the holes.

Fashion and install the decorative centerpiece

1. From 1¹⁄₁₆" oak stock, cut two pieces 6" wide by 22" long. Joint or plane one edge of each piece and then edge-join the pieces together to form the centerpiece (P). Transfer the full-sized pattern outline and heart

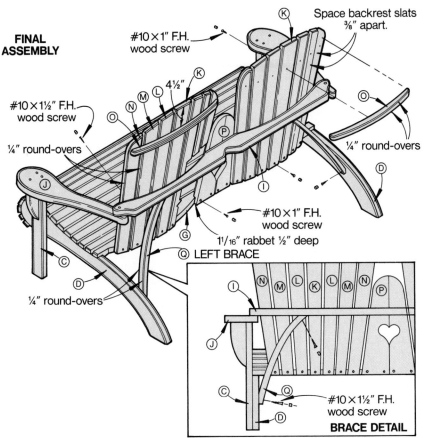

FINAL ASSEMBLY

#10 × 1" F.H. wood screw

Space backrest slats ⅜" apart.

#10 × 1½" F.H. wood screw

¼" round-overs

4½"

¼" round-overs

¼" round-overs

#10 × 1" F.H. wood screw

1¹⁄₁₆" rabbet ½" deep

Q LEFT BRACE

¼" round-overs

#10 × 1½" F.H. wood screw

BRACE DETAIL

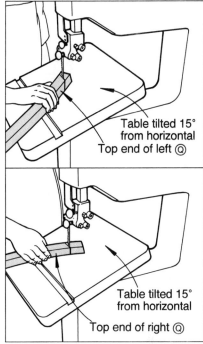

Table tilted 15° from horizontal
Top end of left Q

Table tilted 15° from horizontal

Top end of right Q

opening from the template to the centerpiece blank.

2. Cut or rout a 1¹⁄₁₆"-wide rabbet ½" deep along the bottom front edge of the centerpiece where shown on the Final Assembly Drawing *above*.

3. Bandsaw the centerpiece outline to shape. Using a ¼" blade on your bandsaw, start at the bottom of the centerpiece, cut through the joint line to the heart outline, and then cut the heart opening to shape.

4. Raise your tablesaw blade 2½" above the table and tilt it 10° from vertical. Using the drawing at *right* for reference, bevel-rip the edges of the centerpiece.

5. Sand a ¼" round-over along the front outside edges (except at the rabbet) on the centerpiece.

6. With a belt sander and then a palm sander, form a smooth curve on the front of the centerpiece.

7. Clamp the centerpiece between the slats. Drill four holes through the centerpiece and into

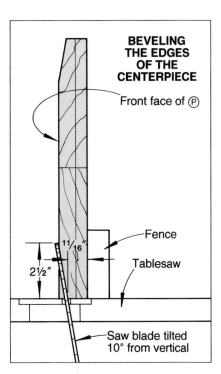

BEVELING THE EDGES OF THE CENTERPIECE

Front face of P

Fence

Tablesaw

1¹⁄₁₆"

2½"

Saw blade tilted 10° from vertical

part G. Mark the hole locations and drill two holes through the centerpiece and into the rear-slat support (I). Screw the centerpiece in place.

Add the braces and apply the finish

1. Cut the braces (Q) to shape. Following the two-step drawing *above*, bandsaw the bevels on the top end of the braces. Rout a ¼" round-over along the edges of both braces.

2. Position the top end of one brace against the rear-slat support (I), and center the lower end on the supports (D) where shown on the Brace Detail *above left*. You'll need to move the brace around until no gap exists between the ends of the brace and the mating surfaces (D, I). Once positioned, tape the brace in place, drill the mounting holes, and fasten it to parts D and I. Repeat the procedure to position and secure the remaining brace.

3. Plug the remaining counterbores. Sand the settee smooth. Finish the settee as desired. (We brushed on several coats of clear Olympic Wood Preservative.)

REDWOOD PATIO TABLE AND BENCHES

This one-of-a-kind hexagonal table design includes six sturdy benches that tuck underneath and together, like slices of a pie, when they're not in use. We selected redwood because it can withstand the sun and rain, and for its beautiful wood tones (which we preserved with a clear wood finish). Don't let all the angle-cutting scare you off. You can do all the top and bench pieces using just a few settings on your saw.

Build the table

Note: Rip ¼" from each edge of all 2×6 stock for a 5" finished width. (This removes the factory-rounded edges, which enables you to make tighter-fitting, better-looking joints.)

1. Cut table leg parts A and B to length. Cut the 45° chamfer on one end of each A as shown on the Table Leg Drawing, page 76.

2. To cut the half-lap joints in leg parts B, start by fitting your saw with a dado blade. Then raise the blade to half the thickness of the redwood stock you are using. Test the depth of cut on scrap of the same thickness as B. Set a stop on the fence 2½" from the blade and cut the half-lap joints on each end of all B pieces.

3. Lay out and mark the stopped half-lap joints on A pieces, 5" in from the squared end as shown in the drawing *below*. We marked the joints in pairs (one top part A and one base part A) for ease and uniformity.

4. With your blade still set at the height used to cut the half-lap joints, set a stop on your saw so that a 2½" notch is cut into one side of each A. (As shown in photo A, *below,* we clamped a stop to the carriage of our radial-arm saw to cut the stopped half-lap joints. You also could use a

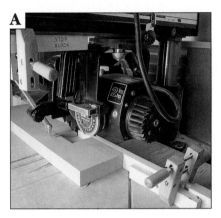

A

router and jig to cut the dado.) Now set a stop on the fence and cut the stopped half-lap joint in six A's, then move the stop on the fence to the other side of the blade and cut the other six A's.

5. Using a router fitted with a straight bit and an edge guide, clean out the stopped half-lap joints as shown in photo B, *top right.* (We set the edge guide so the straight bit would not cut more than 2½" in from the edge. While the guide prevents you from cutting too far in, you will need to clamp on stops for the side cuts—or just eyeball it. You can use this same routing process to cut the entire stopped half lap if you don't want to use the radial-arm saw.) Clean out the two rounded corners of each recess with a mallet and chisel.

B

Check the fit of the half-lap joint of each B into the stopped half-lap joint of each A.

6. Mix the epoxy and brush it onto the mating surfaces of two A's and one B. (To ensure adequate adhesion when brushing epoxy onto the end grain, we applied a first coat, then did the second coat just before clamping and screwing.) Clamp two A's to each B and check for square. Countersink and install two #12×1¼" wood screws into each half-lap joint. The head of the screw should rest just below the surface of the redwood so you won't hit it when sanding later. Set the assembly aside to dry and make five more legs.

7. Sand each assembly smooth with 80-grit paper and use a ¼" round-over bit to rout all the edges except the top edge of the top A piece.

8. With a hacksaw, cut 12 pieces of 1×1×⅛" aluminum angle to 29". Cut the ends of six pieces at 30°, then cut the ends of the other six at 30°, as shown on the Angle for Table Drawing *below.* The pieces join *continued*

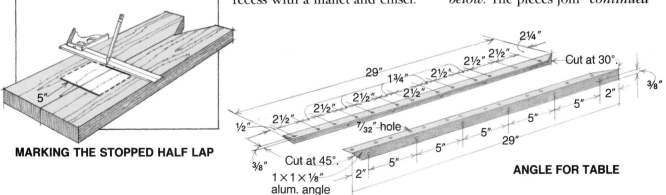

MARKING THE STOPPED HALF LAP

ANGLE FOR TABLE

REDWOOD PATIO TABLE AND BENCHES
continued

at a 60° angle when later mounted to the bottom side of the tabletop. Chamfer the outer ends at 45° in the same manner, matching the chamfer profile on the outside ends of part A.

9. Clamp the aluminum pieces together and lay out the screw holes as dimensioned on the Angle for Table Drawing, page 75. Drill two 7/32″ holes through the angle for each 2×4. Now drill six 7/32″ holes in each 2×4 to mount the angle to the upper part A of the A–B assembly. File or sand all sharp edges and burrs from the angle pieces.

10. Using #10×1¼″ panhead sheet-metal screws, fasten the aluminum supports to both sides of all upper A's. (Use a 2×4 scrap to position the aluminum supports the precise thickness of D below the top edge.)

11. Construct each core block (C) by cutting and laminating with epoxy two 12″ pieces of 2×4. After the epoxy dries, cut the block to 3¼×2¾″ as dimensioned on the Cutting the

Cutting Diagram

14 pieces—2×4×8′ Redwood

13 pieces—2×6×8′ Redwood

¾×24×24″ Exterior Plywood

EXPLODED VIEW

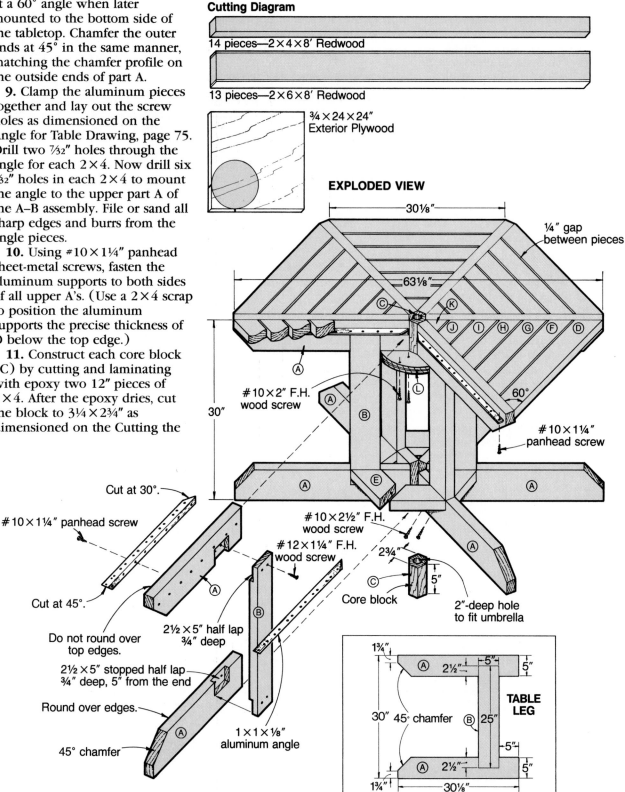

¼″ gap between pieces

30⅛″

63⅛″

#10×2″ F.H. wood screw

#10×1¼″ panhead screw

60°

30″

#10×2½″ F.H. wood screw

#12×1¼″ F.H. wood screw

2¾″

5″

Core block

2″-deep hole to fit umbrella

Cut at 30°.

#10×1¼″ panhead screw

Cut at 45°.

Do not round over top edges.

2½×5″ half lap ¾″ deep

2½×5″ stopped half lap ¾″ deep, 5″ from the end

Round over edges.

45° chamfer

1×1×⅛″ aluminum angle

1¾″

2½″

5″

5″

30″ 45° chamfer 25″

5″

2½″

1¾″

30⅛″

TABLE LEG

Bill of Materials

Part	Finished Size* T	W	L	Mat.	Qty.
Table					
A leg	1⅝"	5"	30⅛"	R	12
B leg	1⅝"	5"	25"	R	6
C core block	2¾"	3¼"	5"	R	2
D top	1⅝"	3½"	30⅛"	R	6
E top	1⅝"	4⅝"	10⅛"	R	6
F top	1⅝"	3½"	25⅞"	R	6
G top	1⅝"	3½"	21½"	R	6
H top	1⅝"	3½"	17⅛"	R	6
I top	1⅝"	3½"	12⅞"	R	6
J top	1⅝"	3½"	8½"	R	6
K top	1⅝"	3½"	4⅛"	R	6
L disc	¾"	12½"	diam.	EP	1
Benches					
M leg	1⅝"	5"	12⅞"	R	24
N leg	1⅝"	5"	16"	R	12
O* rail	1⅝"	3½"	17⅜"	R	6
P seat	1⅝"	3½"	16⅝"	R	6
Q seat	1⅝"	3½"	21"	R	6
R seat	1⅝"	3½"	25⅜"	R	6

*Part marked with an * is cut larger initially, then trimmed to finished size. Please read the instructions before cutting.

Material Key: R—redwood, EP—exterior plywood.
Supplies: epoxy, #12×1¼" flathead wood screws, #10×1¼" panhead sheet-metal screws, #8×2½" flathead wood screws, #10×2" flathead wood screws, #10×3" flathead wood screws, 6—6' pieces of 1×1×⅛" aluminum angle (manufactured by Macklanburg-Duncan and available at most hardware stores), clear exterior finish.
Note: Use all stainless-steel screws for this project, if available.

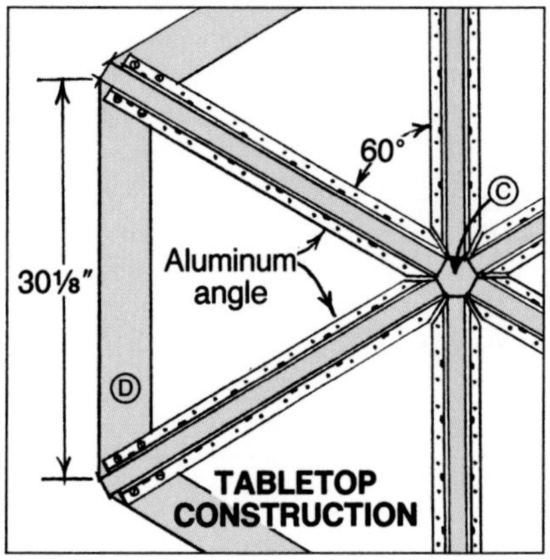

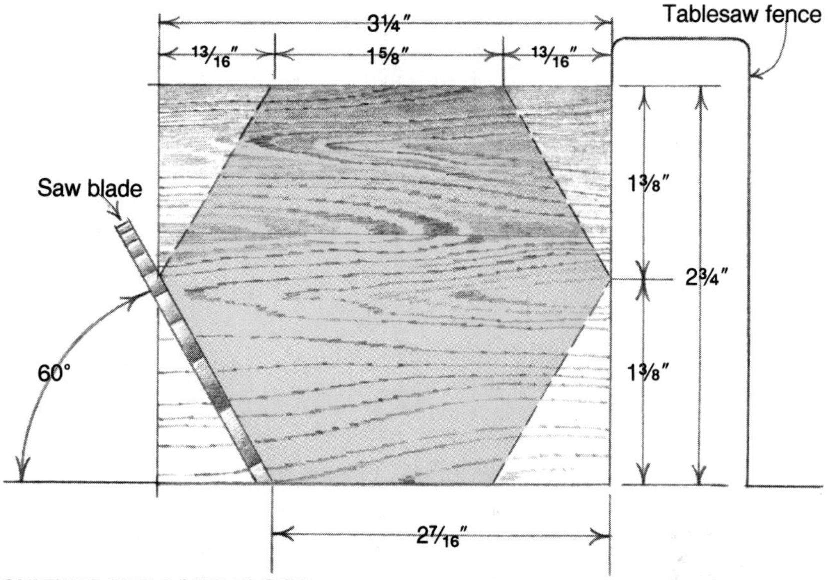

CUTTING THE CORE BLOCK

Core Block Drawing *above.* Now tilt the blade at 60° and set the fence 2 7/16" away from the base of the blade as illustrated on the Cutting the Core Block Drawing. Crosscut the two 5" C blocks from the 12" lamination. If you plan to outfit the table with an umbrella, now's the time to bore a hole completely through the center of the top block and 2" deep into the base block.

Assemble the base

1. Working on a large, flat surface, set all six leg assemblies upside down to form a rough hexagon. Set one core block in the center of the legs. Use a band clamp to position and align the legs around the block. Repeat this with the other block.

2. Set your saw to cut a 60° angle and cut one lineal piece of scrap into six equal lengths. Form a hexagon with the pieces to verify the angle. Miter-cut all six D pieces at 60° to finished length and position them as shown on the Tabletop Construction Drawing, *left.* Slide the pieces under the aluminum and check that they true up the hexagon snugly; trim, if necessary. Using #10×1¼" panhead screws, fasten each D to the aluminum angle on the A–B assembly.

3. Miter-cut parts E to finished length. Then clamp handscrews to B to hold each flush with the top of A, drill pilot holes, and toe-screw each E to the A–B assembly as shown in photo C, page 78.

4. Toe-screw the base core block (C) in place (drive the screws at an angle from the bottom edge of A into the core block).

5. With a helper, turn the table right side up and miter-cut one each of F, G, H, I, J, and K to finished length. Set the pieces into position on the aluminum angle and check for a good fit at the ends and for the ¼" gap between pieces. (We ripped scrap stock to ¼", then crosscut to 2", to form spacers. Then, to assure consistent spacing, we positioned the tabletop pieces in one of the hexagonal sections with the spacers in place.) Now miter-cut the rest of the tabletop pieces to the same lengths.

continued

REDWOOD PATIO TABLE AND BENCHES
continued

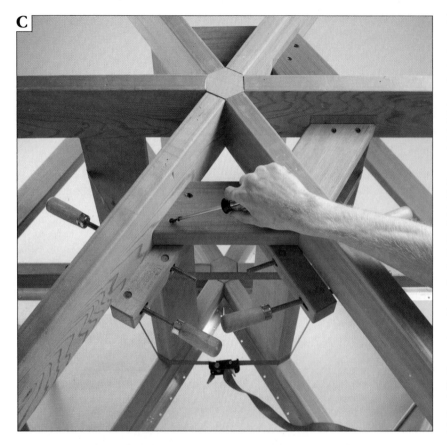

6. Fasten the tabletop pieces (F, G, H, I, J, K) to the aluminum angle, starting with F and working in. Use scrap spacers or a measure to keep a consistent ¼" gap between the pieces.

7. Cut a 12½"-diameter disc (L) from ¾" exterior plywood to fit between the legs for additional stability in the base. Waterproof L with a coat of epoxy and position it while the epoxy is still wet. (Brushing on a coat of epoxy is a quick and simple way of sealing the plywood.) Fasten L to the bottom of the tabletop center with #10×2" wood screws. Now epoxy the upper hexagonal block

C in place and, using it as a guide, bore a hole through the plywood for the umbrella.

8. Sand the entire table assembly smooth with 100-grit sandpaper. Remember that people will come in contact with table and bench surfaces, so be extra careful to sand any sharp edges remaining on these pieces. (We had a few gouges that we filled with a mixture of FIX Wood Patch and cherry stain to match the redwood. We belt-sanded any rough spots with 80-grit sandpaper, then finish-sanded with a pad sander and 100-grit sandpaper.)

Build the benches

Note: Many of the construction techniques used in building the table are repeated in the benches. Refer back, if necessary.

1. Lay out and cut the half-lap joints in the M and N pieces. Chamfer the outside ends of the M pieces to match those of the table legs.

2. Epoxy and screw the bench supports together, positioning the screws so that they are not in the path of the dado to be cut in step 6, below. After the epoxy dries, sand the assemblies smooth with 80-grit sandpaper. Then round over all edges of the assemblies, *except* the top inside edge of each, with a router and a ¼" round-over bit.

3. Rip and crosscut stock for the rails (O) to length plus 2".

4. Cut 12 pieces of aluminum angle to 12". Lay out the hole sequence on the aluminum angle, then drill the holes as dimensioned on the Angle for Bench Drawing, *opposite.*

5. Cut dadoes in each leg. To do this, you'll need to make an auxiliary fence. First tilt the tablesaw blade to 30°, then bevel-rip one edge of a 24"-long scrap 2×4. Glue and nail the smaller of the two resulting pieces onto the other one and fasten the assembly to a miter gauge.

6. Remove the saw blade and insert a dado blade. Set the blade perpendicular with the table and raise it above the surface of the table the thickness of O. Mark the location of the dadoes in the M–N assemblies. Position one assembly against the auxiliary miter-gauge fence with the inside of the assembly facing out. Nail stops to each end of the miter-gauge fence to ensure a finished dado 3½"

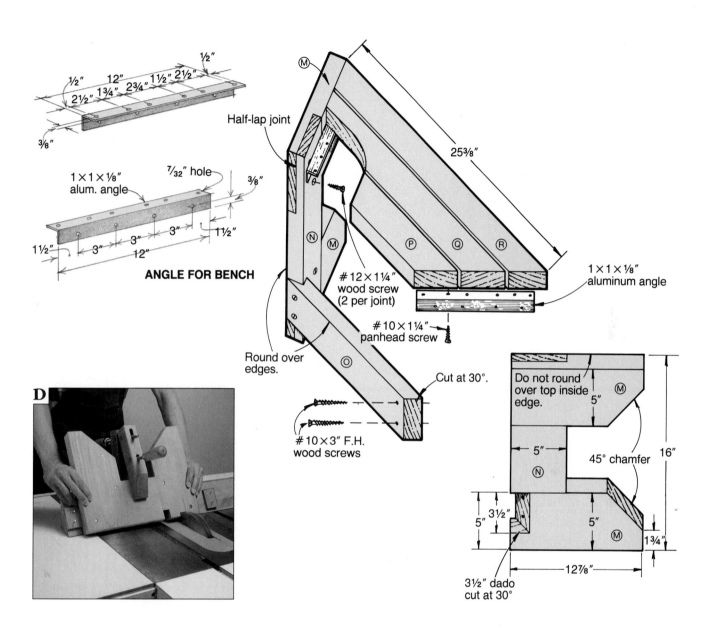

½"
12"
1½" 2½"
½"
2½"
1¾"
2¾"
1½"
⅜"

1×1×⅛"
alum. angle
7/32" hole
⅜"
1½"
1½"
3"
3"
3"
3"
12"
ANGLE FOR BENCH

Half-lap joint

M

25⅜"

N

M

P Q R

#12×1¼"
wood screw
(2 per joint)

#10×1¼"
panhead screw

1×1×⅛"
aluminum angle

Round over
edges.

O

Cut at 30°.

#10×3" F.H.
wood screws

D

Do not round
over top inside
edge.

M

5"

5"

45° chamfer

N

16"

5"
3½"

5"

M

1¾"

3½" dado
cut at 30°

12⅞"

wide. Then cut six of the dadoes to size as shown in photo D, *above,* making sure the screws are not in the path of the cut. Now remove the fence from the miter gauge and move it to the slot on the other side of the blade. Reposition and reattach the fence to cut the other six dadoes.

7. Attach the angle to the M–N assemblies.

8. Miter-cut bench parts P, Q, and R to size and fasten to the aluminum angle.

9. Epoxy and screw the O pieces into the dadoes using two #10×3" wood screws at each joint. After the epoxy dries, use a handsaw to trim the ends of each O flush with the outside edge of the leg assembly.

10. File or sand all sharp edges and burrs from the aluminum, then sand the benches smooth.

Finish the table and benches

1. Apply redwood exterior finish to the table and benches. (We applied several applications of CWF Clear Wood Finish, a penetrating oil. It's made with Penetrol by the Flood Company and is available at many local lumberyards and paint stores. CWF should be renewed about every six months.)

CEDAR-SIDED PLANTERS

Blooming beauties rise to the occasion in these outdoor decorators. Simple to construct, the framework consists of 2×4 stock handsomely covered with weather-resistant cedar fencing. Each planter has a shelf you can position to elevate your favorite plants to just the right height. What better way to display flowers and greenery?

Note: The following directions and photographs—as well as the illustrations on this page and the next one, the Bill of Materials on page 82, and portions of the Cutting Diagram on page 83—are for the medium-height planter. To build the tall and short planters, which vary only slightly from the medium-height planter, see the instructions at the end of the article on page 84, and the illustrations and Bills of Materials on pages 83 and 84.

Construct the skeleton framework

1. Cut four uprights (A) and eight cross members (B) to the sizes listed in the Bill of Materials, page 82. (We ripped and crosscut the uprights to size from one 8′ pressure-treated fir 2×4.)

2. Clamp two cross members between two uprights as shown on the drawing *below*. Check for square, drill ⅛″ pilot holes, and screw the frame together. Repeat for the second frame.

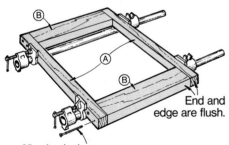

3″ galv. deck screw

3. Clamp the remaining four cross members between the two assembled frames. Now drill pilot holes, and screw them in place as shown in photo A, *right*.

continued

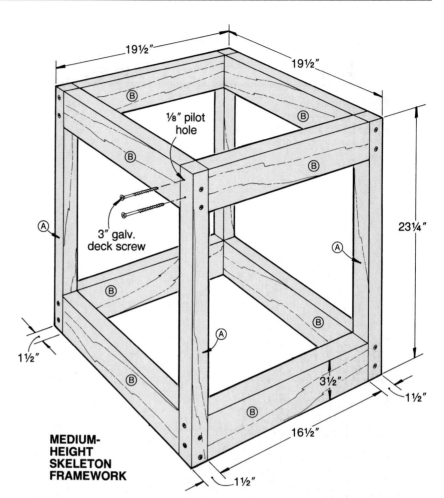

MEDIUM-HEIGHT SKELETON FRAMEWORK

Construct the two frames, clamp the cross members between them, and screw the cross members in position with 3″ deck screws.

CEDAR-SIDED PLANTERS
continued

Bill of Materials				
Part	**Finished Size***		**Mat.**	**Qty.**
	T	**W**	**L**		
Medium-Height Planter					
A upright	1½"	1½"	23¼"	TF	4
B cross member	1½"	3½"	16½"	TF	8
C corner siding	¾"	3½"	23¼"	C	8
D* center siding	¾"	3½"	23¼"	C	16
E* base	¾"	5¼"	22½"	C	4
F* top trim	¾"	2¾"	22½"	C	4
G* top	¾"	3½"	22½"	C	4
H shelf cleat	1½"	1½"	19¼"	TF	2
I shelf board	¾"	5¼"	19¼"	C	3

*Parts marked with an * are cut larger initially, then trimmed to finished size. Please read the instructions before cutting.

Material Key: TF—treated fir, C—cedar.
Supplies: 3" galvanized deck screws, #7 galvanized nails.

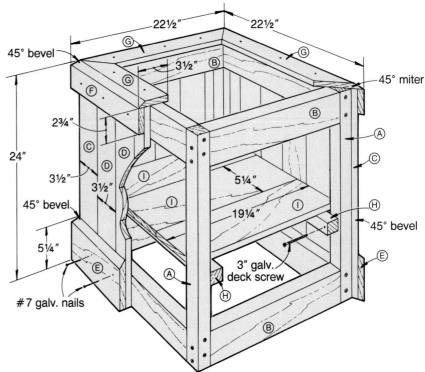

MEDIUM-HEIGHT PLANTER

Nail on the siding

1. Cut eight corner siding pieces (C) and the center siding pieces (D) to length. (We used 1×6×8' cedar fencing. In checking sources, we found that 1×6 cedar fencing varies from 5¼" to 5½" in width. With this in mind, 5¼" is the widest board you'll find on these planters.)

2. Bevel-rip one edge of each corner siding piece at 45° to obtain the finished width (we did this on the tablesaw).

3. Holding the beveled edges tight, nail two corner siding pieces to each corner of the framework. Keep the top edges of the siding pieces flush with the top of the framework. (See the Medium-Height Planter Drawing, *top right,* for details.)

4. Measure the distance between the corner siding pieces (C), divide this distance by 4, and rip each center siding piece (D) to this width plus ⅛" (we cut our pieces to 3⅝" wide).

After assembling the skeleton frame, nail the siding pieces in place by starting at the outside and working in. Plane the center piece to fit.

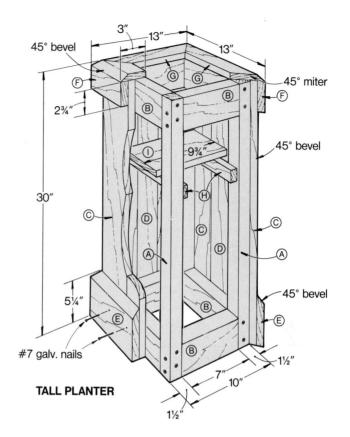

Bill of Materials

Part	Finished Size*			Mat.	Qty.
	T	W	L		
Tall Planter					
A upright	1½"	1½"	29¼"	TF	4
B cross member	1½"	3½"	7"	TF	8
C corner siding	¾"	3¾"	29¼"	C	8
D* center siding	¾"	4"	29¼"	C	4
E* base	¾"	5¼"	13"	C	4
F* top trim	¾"	2¾"	13"	C	4
G* top	¾"	3"	13"	C	4
H shelf cleat	¾"	1½"	9¾"	C	2
I shelf board	¾"	5¼"	9¾"	C	1

*Parts marked with an * are cut larger initially, then trimmed to finished size. Please read the instructions before cutting.

Material Key: TF—treated fir, C—cedar.
Supplies: 3" galvanized deck screws, #7 galvanized nails.

TALL PLANTER

Next, starting at the outside and working in, as shown in photo B, *opposite,* nail the center pieces in place. Plane one edge of each of the last two remaining inside pieces until they fit snugly between the other pieces.

5. Belt-sand the top and bottom edges of the siding (C, D) flush with the top and bottom edges of the framework (A, B).

Cut and add the trim pieces

1. Cut the base pieces (E) to length plus 1".

2. Holding the pieces in place, mark the length needed (a combination square works well for marking the 45° angles). Miter-cut both ends of each base piece. (We cut ours on the tablesaw using a miter gauge to push the pieces over the angled blade. You also could cut the pieces on the radial-arm saw.)

3. Bevel-rip the top edge of each base piece at 45° to trim the board to width. *continued*

Cutting Diagram

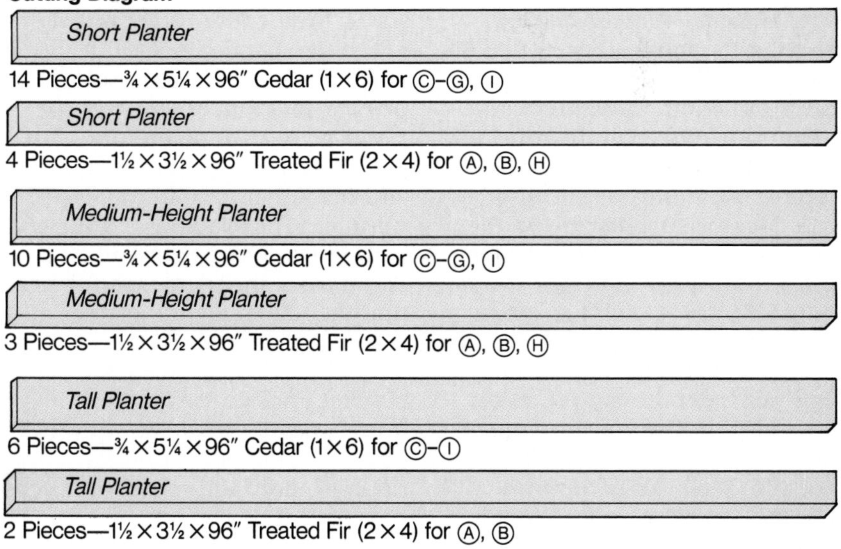

Short Planter

14 Pieces—¾ × 5¼ × 96" Cedar (1×6) for Ⓒ-Ⓖ, Ⓘ

Short Planter

4 Pieces—1½ × 3½ × 96" Treated Fir (2 × 4) for Ⓐ, Ⓑ, Ⓗ

Medium-Height Planter

10 Pieces—¾ × 5¼ × 96" Cedar (1×6) for Ⓒ-Ⓖ, Ⓘ

Medium-Height Planter

3 Pieces—1½ × 3½ × 96" Treated Fir (2 × 4) for Ⓐ, Ⓑ, Ⓗ

Tall Planter

6 Pieces—¾ × 5¼ × 96" Cedar (1×6) for Ⓒ-Ⓘ

Tall Planter

2 Pieces—1½ × 3½ × 96" Treated Fir (2 × 4) for Ⓐ, Ⓑ

CEDAR-SIDED PLANTERS
continued

Bill of Materials				
Part	**Finished Size***			**Mat.**	**Qty.**
	T	**W**	**L**		
Short Planter					
A upright	1½"	1½"	17¼"	TF	4
B cross member	1½"	3½"	27½"	TF	8
C corner siding	¾"	4"	17¼"	C	8
D* center siding	¾"	4"	17¼"	C	24
E* base	¾"	5¼"	33½"	C	4
F* top trim	¾"	2¾"	33½"	C	4
G* top	¾"	3½"	33½"	C	4
H shelf cleat	1½"	1½"	30¼"	TF	2
I shelf board	¾"	5¼"	30¼"	C	5

*Parts marked with an * are cut larger initially, then trimmed to finished size. Please read the instructions before cutting.

Material Key: TF—treated fir, C—cedar.
Supplies: 3" galvanized deck screws, #7 galvanized nails.

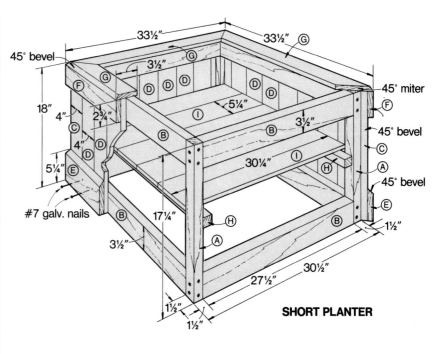

SHORT PLANTER

Nail the pieces in place around the perimeter of the base.

4. Mark the lengths needed, and cut the top trim pieces (F) to length plus 1". Now rip the pieces to width, then miter-cut them to length. Nail the trim pieces in place, flush with the tops of the siding.

5. Measure the distance, and cut the top pieces (G) to length plus 2". Now bevel-rip the outside edge of each piece to trim the piece to a 3½" width. Carefully measure the distance, and miter-cut the top pieces to length. With the outside edge of each top piece (G) flush with the outside face of each top trim piece (F), nail the top pieces in place.

Add the shelf

Note: The shelf allows you to raise or lower your potted plants for the best viewing height. We positioned our shelf so the top of the pot was about level with the top of the planter.

1. Rip and crosscut the shelf cleats (H) to size from 2×4 stock. Now cut the shelf boards (I) to size.

2. To locate the shelf in the planter, measure down from the top edge of each planter the height of the flowerpot plus ¾", and mark that location on each upright. (For example, if your pot is 8" high, measure down 8¾" and make a mark on each upright.) Then lay the planter on its side, position the top edge of one cleat (H) even with the marked lines on two of the uprights, and screw the cleat in place. Lay the planter on its opposite side, and repeat to fasten the second cleat.

3. Lay the shelf boards on the cleats (we didn't nail ours in place in case we ever wanted to change the cleat positions for new pots), then add the plants.

Short planter

To build the shortest of the three planters, refer to the Bill of

Materials, *above left*; the Cutting Diagram, page 83; and the directions for the medium-height planter starting on page 81. Although the sizes of the parts vary between the short and medium-height planters, the lettering of the parts is the same, and the building procedure is nearly identical.

Tall planter

To build the tallest of the three planters, refer to the Bill of Materials and the Cutting Diagram on page 83, and the directions for the medium-height planter starting on page 81. The parts for the tall planter are lettered the same as they are for the medium-height planter, and the building procedure is nearly identical. Note, however, that because of the small opening at the top of the tall planter, you should attach the cleats (H) before attaching the siding.

TEAK DIRECTOR'S CHAIR

For this design, we chose teak, a wood with the reputation for being able to stand up well to the weather. It's been used for centuries in the boat-building business with great success. And because deck furniture typically gets lots of use, we specified mortise-and-tenon joinery and slow-set epoxy. You won't have to worry about these joints coming apart!

Note: The instructions, photographs, and illustrations that follow, as well as the Bill of Materials on page 87, describe how to build a single chair. When making additional chairs, we suggest you cut and laminate all identical pieces at the same time to ensure uniformity. We also recommend that you use a stop when cutting the numerous pieces to length.

Cut pieces to length and width for the side and leg assemblies

Note: For perfectly centered mortises and tenons, it's important to start with stock exactly ¾" thick. Buy stock this thick, or plane thicker stock to this size.

1. From ¾"-thick teak, rip and crosscut eight pieces 1¾ × 16½" long. (We used a stop clamped to the radial-arm-saw fence for consistent lengths.) You'll use four pieces for laminating the two backrest supports (A) and four for the two armrests (B). For ease in mating the teak parts later, label the parts A and B. Cut and label four pieces 1¾ × 16" long for the two lower supports (C) and four pieces 1¾ × 9" long for the two front supports (D).

2. From ¾" teak, rip and crosscut four pieces 1¾ × 16" long. You'll use two of these for the top inner leg (E) *continued*

TEAK DIRECTOR'S CHAIR
continued

and two for the top outer leg (F). Then cut eight pieces $1\frac{3}{4} \times 24\frac{1}{2}''$ long for the inner- and outer-leg supports (G). Next, cut two pieces $1\frac{3}{4} \times 12\frac{3}{8}''$.long for the lower inner-leg spacer (H) and two pieces $1\frac{3}{4} \times 15\frac{1}{2}''$ for the outer-leg spacer (I). Label the teak pieces (E, F, G, H, I) for ease in mating when epoxying later.

Cut the dadoes and rout the coves to form the fabric groove

Note: For perfectly square mortises, we cut dadoes in the individual teak pieces. Then we laminated the pieces together and aligned the dadoes. This method worked better than drilling and chiseling the mortises to shape after laminating the pieces.

1. Mark the location, and cut a $\frac{5}{8}''$ dado $\frac{5}{16}''$ deep in all the parts (except D, H, and I) where dimensioned on the Side Assembly, Inner Leg Assembly, and Outer Leg Assembly drawings *below* and *opposite*. (We cut ours on the radial-arm saw fitted with a dado blade, and clamped a stop to the fence to assure accurately placed dadoes.)

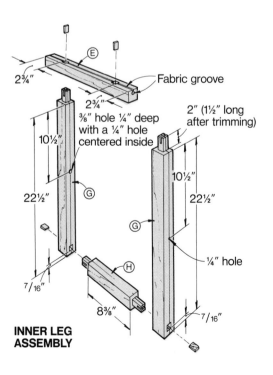

STEP 4. Complete routing chamfer.

STEP 2. Mark an extension of the router chamfer line.

STEP 1. Chamfer inside edges.

STEP 3. Rout to marked line.

CHAMFER DETAIL

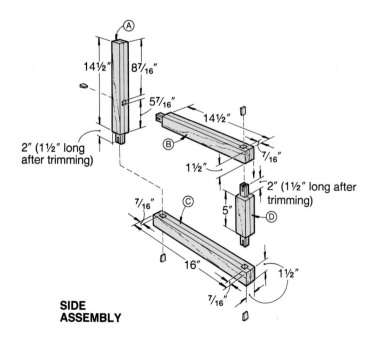

#6 × ½" F.H. brass wood screw (to hold the backrest in place)

Do not chamfer ends.

#6 finish washer

Stop chamfer here.

1½"

⅝" chamfers

Stop chamfers here.

Filler blocks 1½" from end

1½ × 2" solid-brass hinge

Do not chamfer ends.

Stop chamfers here.

EXPLODED VIEW

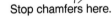

14½"   8⁷⁄₁₆"

5⁷⁄₁₆"

14½"

7⁄₁₆"

2" (1½" long after trimming)

1½"

7⁄₁₆"

2" (1½" long after trimming)

5"

16"

7⁄₁₆"   1½"

7⁄₁₆"

SIDE ASSEMBLY

2¾"

2¾"

Fabric groove

⅜" hole ¼" deep with a ¼" hole centered inside

2" (1½" long after trimming)

10½"

22½"

10½"

22½"

¼" hole

7⁄₁₆"

8⅜"

7⁄₁₆"

INNER LEG ASSEMBLY

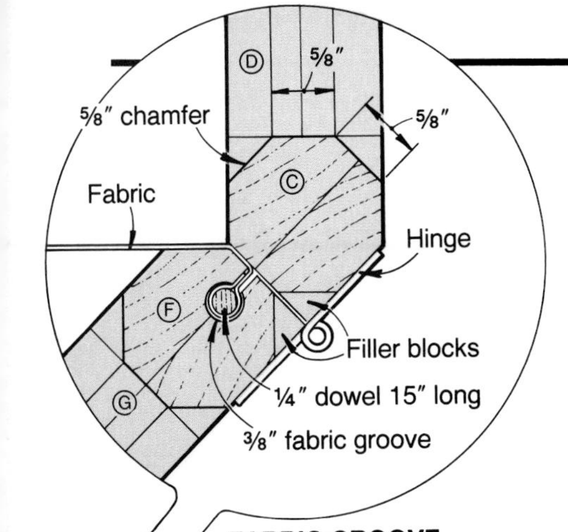
⅝" chamfer
D
⅝"
⅝"
C
Fabric
Hinge
F
Filler blocks
G
¼" dowel 15" long
⅜" fabric groove

FABRIC GROOVE DETAIL

Cutting Diagram

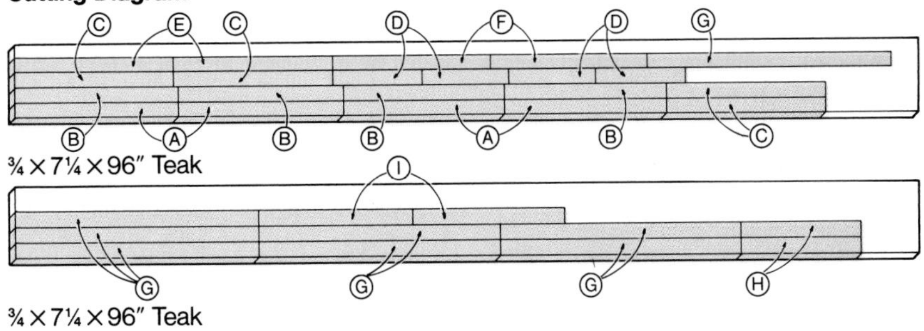
C E C D F D G
B A B B A B C
¾×7¼×96" Teak
I
G G G H
¾×7¼×96" Teak

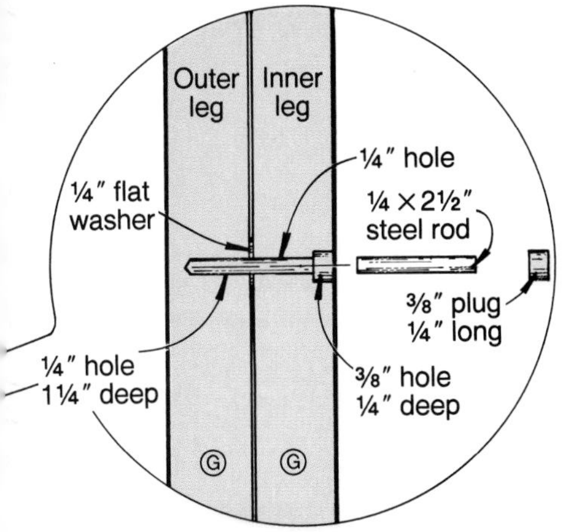
Outer leg
Inner leg
¼" hole
¼ × 2½" steel rod
¼" flat washer
⅜" plug ¼" long
¼" hole 1¼" deep
⅜" hole ¼" deep
G
G

SECTION VIEW PIVOT PIN DETAIL

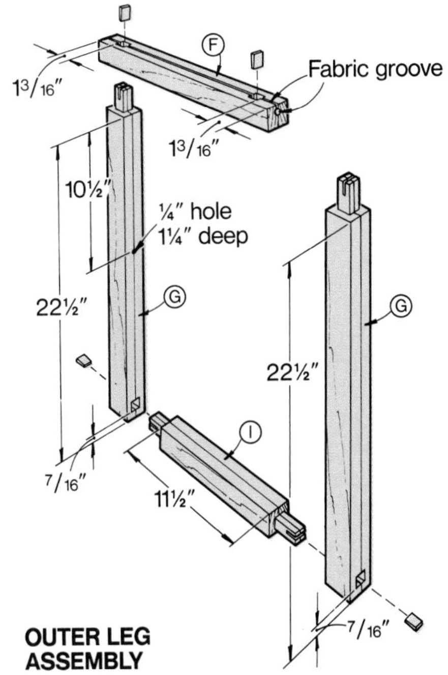
F
Fabric groove
1³/16"
1³/16"
10½"
¼" hole 1¼" deep
22½"
G
22½"
G
I
7/16"
11½"
7/16"

OUTER LEG ASSEMBLY

Bill of Materials					
Part	Initial Sizes* T	W	L	Mat.	Qty.
Side Assemblies					
A* backrest support	1¾"	1½"	16½"	T	2
B* armrest	1¾"	1½"	16½"	T	2
C* lower support	1¾"	1½"	16"	T	2
D* front support	1¾"	1½"	9"	T	2
Inner- and Outer-Leg Assemblies					
E* top inner leg	1¾"	1½"	16"	T	1
F* top outer leg	1¾"	1½"	16"	T	1
G* leg support	1¾"	1½"	24½"	T	4
H* leg spacer	1¾"	1½"	12⅜"	T	1
I* leg spacer	1¾"	1½"	15½"	T	1

*The sizes listed are the sizes of the laminations before they are trimmed to 1½" wide and the wedged tenons are trimmed.

Material Key: T—teak (laminated).
Supplies: latex gloves, 2—¼"-diameter by 2½"-long steel pins (cut from ¼"-diameter steel rod), 2—¼" flat washers, 4—1½ × 2" solid-brass hinges (Stanley part no. CD5304), ¼"-thick clear acrylic for router base (optional), fabric recommended for outdoor use (see the drawings for size), 2—#6 × ½" flathead brass wood screws and brass finishing washers, 2—¼ × 15"-long oak dowel stock, alcohol, paraffin, slow-set epoxy, finish.

2. To form the fabric groove in the top inner- and outer-leg parts (E, F), rout a ⅜" cove 3⁄16" deep the length of each upper-leg part where shown on the drawing immediately *below*.

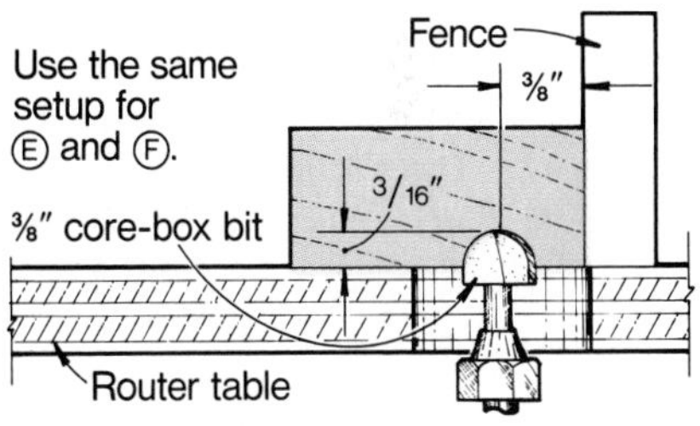
Fence
⅜"
Use the same setup for E and F.
3/16"
⅜" core-box bit
Router table

Laminate the teak pieces, then trim them to width and length

1. Thoroughly mix slow-set epoxy. (For better adhesion, we wiped the mating teak surfaces with alcohol before applying the epoxy. When working with the alcohol and epoxy, we wore latex gloves and applied epoxy to the teak with a 1"-wide nylon brush.)

2. Spread epoxy on the mating surfaces, keeping the epoxy about ¼" away from the dadoes and fabric grooves. With the dadoes and grooves aligned and the edges and ends flush, clamp each assembly (for convenience, we used spring clamps).

If some epoxy seeps into the fabric grooves, ream the grooves with a 20"-long length of ¼"-diameter threaded rod or dowel stock. (To keep *continued*

TEAK DIRECTOR'S CHAIR
continued

the fabric grooves aligned, we spread paraffin on ⅜ × 1"-long dowels. The paraffin prevents the dowels from being epoxied into place. Then we pushed each dowel about ¼" into each end of the fabric grooves.) *Double-check that the dadoes did not come out of alignment when you clamped the assemblies.* Realign, if necessary, and immediately wipe off any excess epoxy.

3. After the epoxy cures for 24 hours, remove the clamps, and scrape any excess epoxy from *one* edge and both ends of each lamination. Use a sharp ½" chisel to remove epoxy from mortises.

4. Plane the *scraped* edge of each chair part. Set the tablesaw fence 1½" from the inside edge of the saw blade. With the *planed* edge against the fence, rip the opposite edge of each chair part to 1½" wide. On parts E and F, cut the edge that is *opposite* the fabric groove.

Form the tenons and slots

1. Measure and make a mark 2" from the bottom end of each part A, the back end of each part B, and the top end of each part G for the 2"-long tenons (see the Side Assembly, Inner Leg Assembly, and Outer Leg Assembly drawings, pages 86 and 87). Repeat the process to mark tenons on *both* ends of parts D, H, and I.

2. Using your radial-arm saw or tablesaw and a stop clamped to the fence, cut the tenons to shape. (We first test-cut a tenon in 1½ × 1½" scrap stock to check the fit of the tenon into the previously cut mortises.) See the Mortise and Tenon Drawing, *above, center,* for dimensions.

3. Bandsaw a ⅛"-wide slot 1⅛" long in each tenon where shown on the Mortise and Tenon Drawing. Notice that the slot is perpendicular to the glue line. You'll need to make a couple of

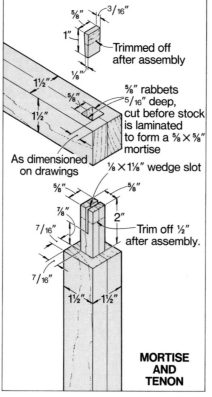

MORTISE AND TENON

passes to form the slot. (To ensure a straight slot, we positioned the chair part against the fence when cutting the slots. We also clamped a stop to the fence to ensure 1⅛"-long cuts.)

Do final machining before joining the parts

1. So that you'll be able to join the inner- and outer-leg assemblies later, drill a ⅜" hole ¼" deep where marked on the inside edge of both inner-leg supports (G). See the Inner Leg Assembly Drawing, page 86, for dimensions and the Section View Pivot Pin Detail accompanying the Exploded View Drawing, pages 86 and 87, for hole sizes. Now drill a ¼" hole through the center of each ⅜" hole.

2. Using the Outer Leg Assembly Drawing, page 87, as a guide, drill a ¼" hole 1¼" deep,

centered from side to side, on the inside edge of each outer-leg support (G).

3. To form the wedges for the tenon slots, start by cutting a piece of teak to ⅝ × 1 × 10" long. Fit your saw table with a zero-clearance insert (we used hardboard). Next, set your tablesaw miter gauge 2° from center, and clamp a spacer block to your tablesaw rip fence where shown on the drawing *below.*

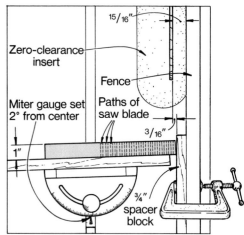

4. Slide the teak piece against the spacer block, push the miter gauge forward, and cut and discard the first piece. Turn the teak piece a half turn, and make the second cut to form the first wedge. Repeat the turning and cutting until you have cut 16 teak wedges.

Join the parts

1. Dry-clamp the assemblies together to check the fit. Position the leg supports (G) correctly to keep the pivot-pin holes facing the right direction. Wipe with alcohol, apply epoxy to the mating surfaces, and clamp the assemblies together.

2. Spread epoxy in the slots, drive the wedges, and check each assembly for square. Scrape off excess epoxy. Let the epoxy cure.

3. Trim the protruding tenons and wedges from each mortise. Sand the joints smooth.

4. When assembling the pieces, the tenons block a section of the fabric groove in each upper-leg part. To open the groove, use the existing groove hole as a guide, and drill a ⅜″ hole through the tenon. (We used a ⅜″ spade bit.)

Kerf the fabric slot and rout the chamfers

1. To finish forming the fabric groove, position the inner-leg assembly on the tablesaw against the fence and directly over the saw blade where shown on the drawing *below.* Cut a ⅛″ kerf the length of the top inner leg (E) and the top outer leg (F).

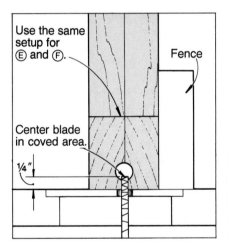

Use the same setup for Ⓔ and Ⓕ.

Fence

Center blade in coved area.

¼″

2. Rout a chamfer along the edges of the side and leg assemblies, lowering the bit each pass to reduce chip-out. Don't rout the ends where shown and described on the four-step Chamfer Detail accompanying the Exploded View Drawing, page 86. (We stopped routing just short of the ends, and sanded the teak parts to finish the chamfers.)

Note: For greater support and a better view when routing, we cut a 12″-diameter disc from ¼″ acrylic. We removed the subbase from our router and mounted the acrylic base in its place.

Cut the pivot pins and filler blocks

1. To make the pivot pins that join the legs, cut two 2½″-long pieces of ¼″-diameter steel rod.

2. To make the filler blocks that support the hinges, bevel-rip the edge of a 20″ length of ¾″ teak to a ½×½″ wedge. Set a stop, and crosscut eight filler blocks, each 1½″ long, from the 20″ length.

3. Mark the positions for the filler blocks where shown on the Exploded View Drawing, and epoxy them to leg pieces E and F and the lower supports (C).

4. Later, plane the filler blocks flush with surfaces of the chair parts as shown in photo A, *below.*

5. Insert the ¼″ steel pins into the pivot-pin holes, and place a ¼″ washer between the leg assemblies (see the Section View Pivot Pin Detail, page 87). Cut two ⅜″-diameter plugs ⁵⁄₁₆″ long, and plug the holes. Sand the chair assemblies smooth.

A

Plane the hinge-support blocks flush with the chamfered edges.

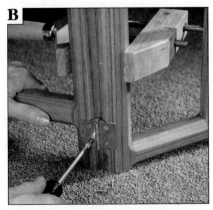

B

Screw the brass hinges to the hinge-support blocks.

Apply the finish and sew the seat and back

1. Apply the finish of your choice. (We used a two-part, marine-grade, penetrating oil).

2. Clamp the chair parts together as shown in photo B, *bottom left,* drill pilot holes, and screw the hinges to the filler blocks and chair parts.

3. Cut a piece of fabric to 18×20½″ for the seat and one piece 8×31⅛″ for the backrest (we used Sunbrella—an awning material; canvas or another material suited for outdoor use also would work). Fold and hem all four edges of the backrest and the front and back edges of the seat, using the drawings *below* as guides. To finish forming the tube-shaped ends on the seat, fold the nonhemmed ends over and sew the edges to the fabric. Repeat the sewing procedure to form the backrest.

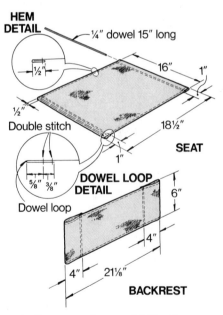

HEM DETAIL
¼″ dowel 15″ long
½″
16″
1″
½″
Double stitch
18½″
SEAT
1″
⁵⁄₈″ ⅜″
Dowel loop
DOWEL LOOP DETAIL
6″
4″
4″ 21⅛″
BACKREST

4. Cut two pieces of ¼″ oak dowel to 15″ long. Insert one dowel in each looped end of the seat. Slide the dowel and fabric into the fabric groove in the top pieces of the leg assemblies. Slip the backrest on and screw it into place where shown on the Exploded View Drawing.

MAHOGANY GARDEN BENCH

Whether you use it outdoors as a fine piece of lawn furniture or indoors as a hall bench, this settee will do the job admirably. The beauty and weather resistance of mahogany, plus the durability of mortise-and-tenon joinery, add up to a sure pleaser.

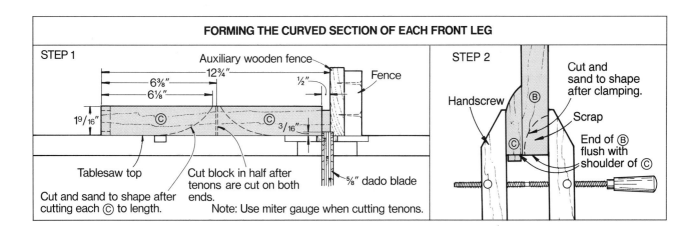

STEP 1

Auxiliary wooden fence

12¾"

6⅜"
6⅛"

½"

Fence

19/16"

C

C

3/16"

Tablesaw top

Cut block in half after tenons are cut on both ends.

⅝" dado blade

Cut and sand to shape after cutting each C to length.

Note: Use miter gauge when cutting tenons.

STEP 2

Cut and sand to shape after clamping.

B

Handscrew

Scrap

C

End of B flush with shoulder of C

Start with the legs

Note: You'll need 2½ × 2½" mahogany for the front and rear legs. You can either laminate thinner stock or special-order 3 × 3" turning squares and cut or plane them to 2½" square. Also, if you plan to use the settee outdoors, be sure to use slow-set epoxy for the adhesive.

1. Rip and crosscut two rear legs (A) and two front legs (B) to the sizes listed in the Bill of Materials, page 93. Chamfer both ends of the rear legs and the bottom end of the front legs. (We chamfered ours on the tablesaw with the blade at 45°.)

2. To shape the curved portion of the front legs (C), refer to the two-step Forming the Curved Section of Each Front Leg Drawing *above,* and start by crosscutting a 12¾" length of 2½"-square mahogany for the curved sections. Rip the piece to a 1⁹⁄₁₆" thickness. Then lay out the two curved sections (including the tenons) on the stock, using the Front Leg Grid, *above right,* as a guide.

3. Mount a dado blade in your tablesaw, and cut a ½" rabbet ³⁄₁₆" deep all the way around each end of the length to form the tenons, as shown on Step 1 of the drawing *above.* Then cut the mahogany blank in half, and cut the two curved sections to shape on the bandsaw. Hand-sand the curved edge of each curved section smooth.

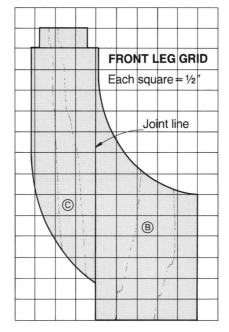

FRONT LEG GRID

Each square = ½"

Joint line

C

B

4. As shown on Step 2 of the drawing, clamp parts B and C together, with the shoulder of the tenon of each curved section (C) flush with the top end of each front-leg member (B). Later, remove the clamps, and lay out the curved shape on the front top edge of each front-leg member (B), using the Front Leg Grid as a guide. Cut to shape and sand.

Form the mortises in the legs

1. Mark the mortise centerpoints on the two rear legs (A) and the two front legs (B) where shown on the Rear Leg and Front Leg drawings, page 93. (Remember that you are working in pairs of A's and Bs, and that

the mortises in one A must be a mirror image of those in the other.) Mark all the mortise centerpoints on each pair before drilling to ensure that you mortise the correct edges of each of the legs.

2. Form the mortises following the multistep sequence outlined on the Mortise Forming Detail accompanying the Rear Leg Drawing.

Cut and tenon the other frame members

1. Cut the side rails (D), center rail (E), and lower rails (F) to the sizes listed in the Bill of Materials. Cut the stretcher (G) to size plus 1" in length. Cut the seat rails (H, I), armrests (J), backrest top (K), and the backrest bottom (L) to size. (Do not make the contour cuts on D, E, and J yet; you'll cut these parts to shape after tenoning.)

2. Cut tenons on both ends of the side rails (D), lower rails (F), seat rails (H, I), the back end of the armrests (J), and both ends of the backrest top and bottom (K, L). Refer to the Side and Center Rail Grid, page 93, for the tenon sizes on the side rails (D). See the Armrest Drawing, page 92, for the tenon size on the armrest, and refer to the details on the Exploded View Drawing, also page 92, for tenon sizes on the backrest top and bottom (K, L). Cut the rest of the tenons

continued

MAHOGANY GARDEN BENCH
continued

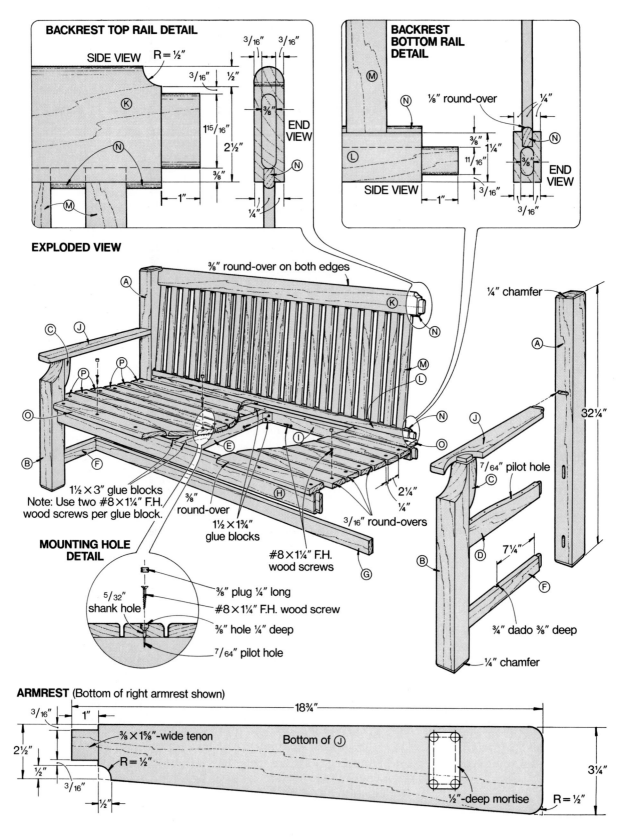

BACKREST TOP RAIL DETAIL

SIDE VIEW R = ½"

3/16" 3/16"

3/16" ½"

Ⓚ

1¹⁵/₁₆"

2½"

Ⓝ

3/8"

3/8"

END VIEW

Ⓝ

Ⓜ

1"

¼"

Ⓝ

EXPLODED VIEW

BACKREST BOTTOM RAIL DETAIL

Ⓜ

Ⓝ

⅛" round-over

¼"

3/8" 1¼"

Ⓛ

11/16"

Ⓝ

3/8"

END VIEW

SIDE VIEW

1"

3/16"

3/16"

⅜" round-over on both edges

Ⓐ

Ⓚ

¼" chamfer

Ⓝ

Ⓒ Ⓙ

Ⓜ

Ⓐ

32¼"

Ⓟ

Ⓟ

Ⓝ

Ⓝ

Ⓛ

Ⓞ

Ⓞ

Ⓙ

Ⓑ Ⓕ

7/64" pilot hole

Ⓔ

Ⓘ

Ⓒ

1½ × 3" glue blocks
Note: Use two #8 × 1¼" F.H. wood screws per glue block.

⅜" round-over

1½ × 1¾" glue blocks

Ⓗ

#8 × 1¼" F.H. wood screws

Ⓖ

2¼"
¼"

3/16" round-overs

Ⓑ

Ⓓ

7¼"

Ⓕ

¾" dado ⅜" deep

¼" chamfer

MOUNTING HOLE DETAIL

5/32" shank hole

⅜" plug ¼" long

#8 × 1¼" F.H. wood screw

⅜" hole ¼" deep

7/64" pilot hole

ARMREST (Bottom of right armrest shown)

3/16" 1"

18¾"

2½"

⅜ × 1⅝"-wide tenon

Bottom of Ⓙ

3¼"

½"

R = ½"

3/16"

½"-deep mortise

R = ½"

½"

Cutting Diagram

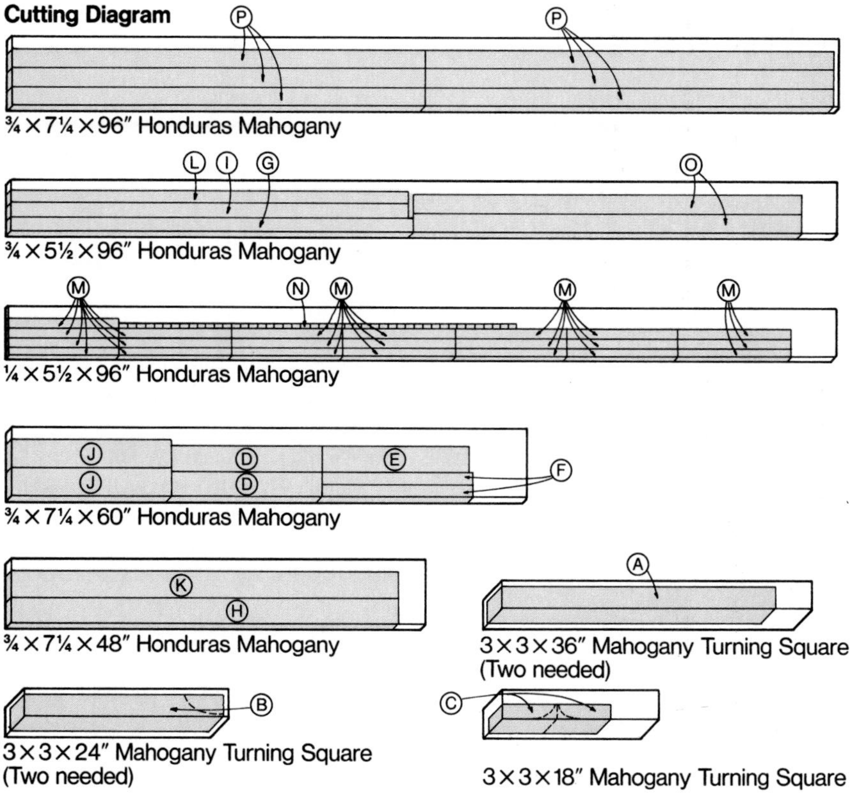

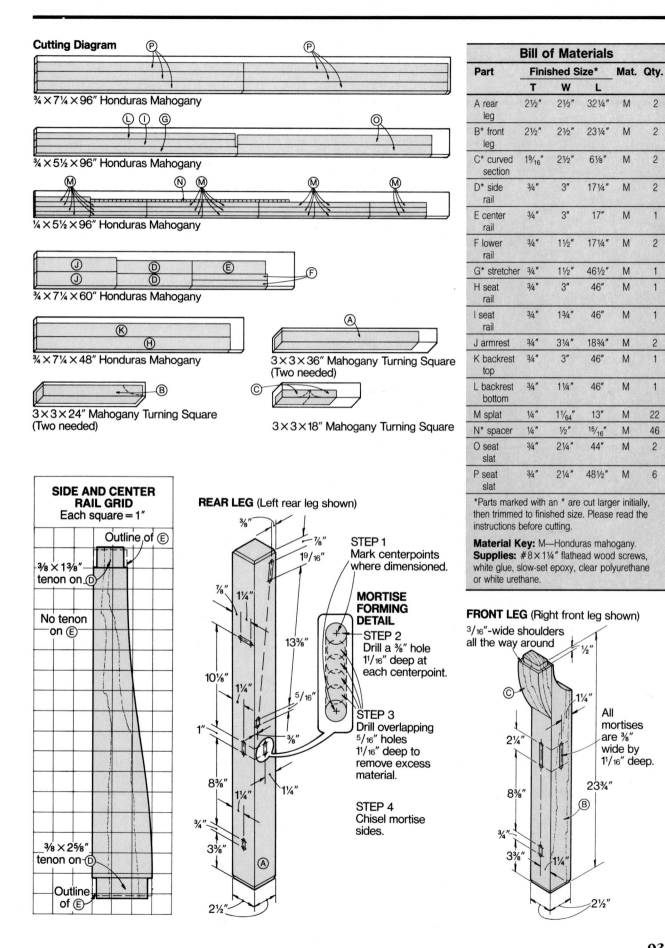

P
P
¾ × 7¼ × 96″ Honduras Mahogany
L
I
G
O
¾ × 5½ × 96″ Honduras Mahogany
M
N
M
M
M
¼ × 5½ × 96″ Honduras Mahogany
J
J
D
D
E
F
¾ × 7¼ × 60″ Honduras Mahogany
K
H
¾ × 7¼ × 48″ Honduras Mahogany
A
3 × 3 × 36″ Mahogany Turning Square (Two needed)
B
3 × 3 × 24″ Mahogany Turning Square (Two needed)
C
3 × 3 × 18″ Mahogany Turning Square

Bill of Materials					
Part	Finished Size*			Mat.	Qty.
	T	W	L		
A rear leg	2½″	2½″	32¼″	M	2
B* front leg	2½″	2½″	23¼″	M	2
C* curved section	1⁹⁄₁₆″	2½″	6⅛″	M	2
D* side rail	¾″	3″	17¼″	M	2
E center rail	¾″	3″	17″	M	1
F lower rail	¾″	1½″	17¼″	M	2
G* stretcher	¾″	1½″	46½″	M	1
H seat rail	¾″	3″	46″	M	1
I seat rail	¾″	1¾″	46″	M	1
J armrest	¾″	3¼″	18¾″	M	2
K backrest top	¾″	3″	46″	M	1
L backrest bottom	¾″	1¼″	46″	M	1
M splat	¼″	1¹⁄₆₄″	13″	M	22
N* spacer	¼″	½″	¹⁵⁄₁₆″	M	46
O seat slat	¾″	2¼″	44″	M	2
P seat slat	¾″	2¼″	48½″	M	6

*Parts marked with an * are cut larger initially, then trimmed to finished size. Please read the instructions before cutting.

Material Key: M—Honduras mahogany.
Supplies: #8 × 1¼″ flathead wood screws, white glue, slow-set epoxy, clear polyurethane or white urethane.

SIDE AND CENTER RAIL GRID
Each square = 1″

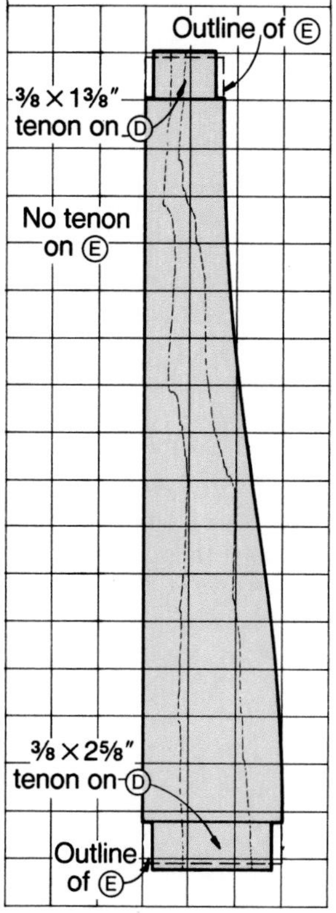

Outline of E
⅜ × 1⅜″ tenon on D
No tenon on E
⅜ × 2⅝″ tenon on D
Outline of E

REAR LEG (Left rear leg shown)

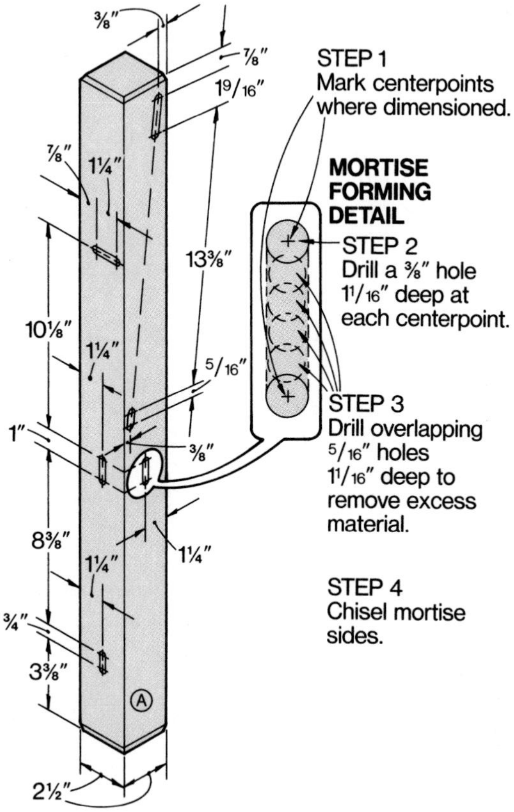

⅜″
⅞″
1⁹⁄₁₆″
⅞″
1¼″
13⅜″
10⅛″
1¼″
5⁄16″
1″
⅜″
8⅜″
1¼″
1¼″
¾″
3⅜″
A
2½″
STEP 1
Mark centerpoints where dimensioned.
MORTISE FORMING DETAIL
STEP 2
Drill a ⅜″ hole 1¹⁄₁₆″ deep at each centerpoint.
STEP 3
Drill overlapping ⁵⁄₁₆″ holes 1¹⁄₁₆″ deep to remove excess material.
STEP 4
Chisel mortise sides.

FRONT LEG (Right front leg shown)

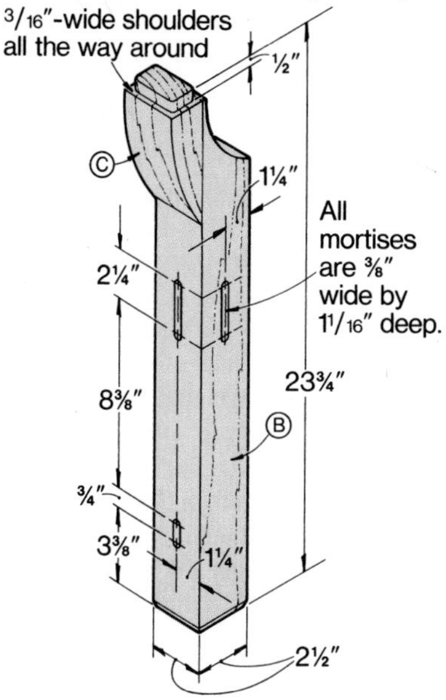

³⁄₁₆″-wide shoulders all the way around
½″
C
1¼″
All mortises are ⅜″ wide by 1¹⁄₁₆″ deep.
2¼″
8⅜″
23¾″
B
¾″
3⅜″
1¼″
2½″

MAHOGANY GARDEN BENCH
continued

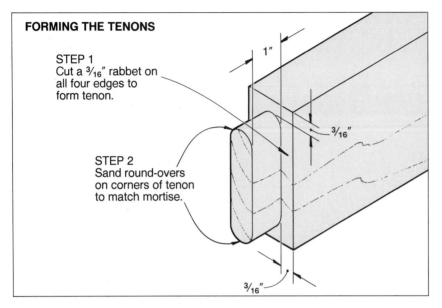

FORMING THE TENONS

STEP 1
Cut a 3/16" rabbet on all four edges to form tenon.

STEP 2
Sand round-overs on corners of tenon to match mortise.

1"

3/16"

3/16"

on the remaining pieces (F, H, I) using the shoulder dimensions noted on the Forming the Tenons Drawing, *above*.

3. Cut a 3/4" dado 3/8" deep in each lower rail (F) where shown on the Exploded View Drawing, page 92.

4. With a bandsaw, cut the side rails (D) and center rail (E) to shape using the Side and Center Rail Grid, page 93.

5. Cut the armrests to final shape using the Armrest Drawing, page 92, as a guide.

Assemble the end sections

1. Dry-clamp the legs (A, B) and rails (D, F) together. Square each assembly, and slide the tenon on the armrest into its mating mortise in the rear leg. Hold the armrest firmly against the tenoned top of the front leg, and mark the location of the mortise needed on the bottom side of each armrest. Now remove the armrest.

2. To form the mortise on the *bottom* side of each armrest, use a flat-bottomed bit and drill a 1/2"-deep hole at each corner of your layout lines. Drill overlapping

holes to remove stock, then chisel the mortise clean.

3. Recheck the fit of the end sections with the armrests in position. Now glue and clamp the end sections together, checking both for square. Position, but *do not* glue, the armrests in their mating parts at this point. You'll glue them later, after the seat slats have been attached.

Complete the frame and build the backrest

1. Dry-clamp the seat rails (H, I) and backrest top and bottom (K, L) between the end assemblies, and check for square. Measure the distance between the dadoes in the lower rails (F), and cut the stretcher (G) to fit this dimension. Finally, remove the clamps and disassemble.

2. Using the Backrest Top Rail Detail accompanying the Exploded View Drawing, page 92, as a guide, cut or rout a 1/4" groove 3/8" deep centered along the bottom edge of the backrest top rail (K) and along the top edge of the bottom rail (L). (We cut ours on the tablesaw fitted with a 1/4" dado blade. We also used a feather board to keep the

pieces firmly against the fence when dadoing.)

3. Rip 11 strips 1 1/64" wide by 13" long from 3/4" mahogany stock. Now resaw each strip to obtain two 1/4 × 1 1/64"-wide strips for the splats (M). (We inserted the backrest top and bottom rails into their mating mortises and measured the length needed for the splats.) To form the spacers (N), start by cutting two strips 1/4 × 1/2 × 30" long. Rout or sand a 1/8" round-over along one edge of each long strip. Now set a stop and cut 46 spacers (plus a few extra) to length (15/16").

4. Measure and mark the lengthwise center of the backrest top rail (K) and the center of one spacer (N). As shown in photo A, *opposite, top,* position the marked spacer in the groove, and align its center mark with the centerline on the backrest top rail. Working from the center out, glue and clamp the splats and spacers in position, checking *each* splat for square. If the spacers on each end extend past the groove, trim them to length.

5. Once you have glued all the spacers and splats in position in the backrest top rail, clamp a scrap strip on each side of the splats to align them as shown in photo B, *opposite, middle.* Now run a bead of glue down the groove in the backrest bottom rail, and tap this part onto the ends of the splats as shown in the photo. As soon as all the splats are positioned in the groove in the bottom rail, flip the assembly over to keep the glue in the groove from running down the splats. Immediately wipe off any excess glue with a wet rag.

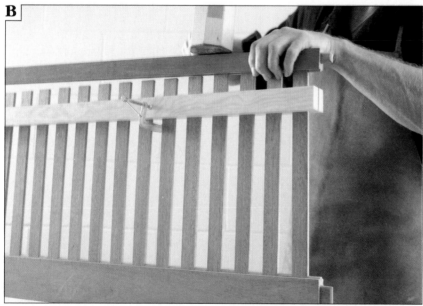

screw the glue blocks to the framework to hold the center rail in position.

3. Cut the seat slats (O, P) to size. Rout a 3⁄16″ round-over along the top edges of each. Cut several strips of scrapwood 1⁄4″ wide for use as spacers. Clamp the front slat (O) to the bench flush with the front edge of the front legs (B). Now work toward the back, spacing the slats 1⁄4″ apart with the scrap spacers.

4. Once all the slats are clamped in position, drill plug, shank, and pilot holes to the sizes indicated on the Mounting Hole Detail accompanying the Exploded View Drawing.

5. Again, starting with the front slat, remove the clamps, and glue and screw the front slat to the bench framework. Proceed toward the back, gluing one slat at a time.

6. Plane a piece of mahogany to a 5⁄16″ thickness, then cut thirty-two 3⁄8″-diameter plugs from it. Plug the screw holes and sand the plugs flush.

7. Glue and clamp the armrests (J) in position.

Finish the bench

1. Sand the settee smooth. Stain and finish as desired. (For indoor use, we finished the settee with clear polyurethane and no stain. For outdoor use, we applied two coats of white exterior urethane.)

6. Again, starting at the center, glue the spacers in position, trimming the end spacers if they protrude. Check the fit of the backrest assembly (K, L, M, N) into the mortises in the rear legs. Separate the backrest assembly from the rear legs.

7. Rout a 3⁄8″ round-over along the top edges of the backrest top rail (K). Then mark and cut a 1⁄2″ radius on each top corner of the backrest top rail. Sand each radius smooth with a 1⁄2″ drum sander.

Build the seat

1. Glue and clamp the seat rails (H, I) and the backrest assembly between the end sections, checking for square.

2. Clamp the center rail (E) between the seat rails, centered from end to end. Cut four triangular glue blocks to the size stated on the Exploded View Drawing. Working with one glue block at a time, hold a block in position against the center rail, and drill 7⁄64″ pilot holes and 5⁄32″ shank holes. Finally, glue and

ACKNOWLEDGMENTS

Project Designers

Dave Ashe—Oak Chair, pages
43–47; Raised-Panel Library Desk,
pages 60–65

James R. Downing—Barrister's
Bookcase, pages 5–9; Stackable
File Cabinet, pages 10–14; Cherry
Curio Cabinet, pages 30–35;
Expandable Oak Dining Table,
pages 37–42; Sunburst Dining
Table, pages 48–53; Redwood
Patio Table and Benches, pages
74–79; Cedar-Sided Planters,
pages 80–84; Teak Director's
Chair, pages 85–89; Mahogany
Garden Bench, pages 90–95

Luis A. Elizondo—Solid-Oak
Settee, pages 67–73

Marlen Kemmet—Arched-Top
Shelving System, pages 22–29;
Oak Herringbone Dining Table,
pages 54–59

Gary Schuknecht—Modular
Entertainment Center, pages
15–21

Photographers

Bob Calmer
Hopkins Associates
Jim Kascoutas

Illustrators

Kim Downing
Randall Foshee
Mike Henry
Bill Zaun